ISBN: 9781903261071

First published: November 2021

By Croft House Consultancy

Following in his footsteps

Arthur Jackson (1912 - 2011)

Contents

Acknowledgements

With the best will in the world I could never have managed to complete this, the first part of *Stepping into the Past* without the generous support of others.

I should like to thank the members of staff at Whaley Bridge Library for their help on my periodic visits. It was a pleasure to work there. The staff at Chester Record Office and at the town libraries in Buxton, Macclesfield and Stockport were also most welcoming. The fascinating material collected by the Whaley Bridge Local History Forum, the Facebook group "Growing Up in Whaley Bridge", and Furness Vale Local History Society was most useful. David Easton has been an inspiration. David Stirling's meticulously researched and attractively presented website goytvalley.org.uk proved very stimulating, too.

I naturally owe a great deal to the labours of William and Joyce Eyre, Allan Shaw and contributors to disley.net like Joyce Winfield. John Sidebottom generously gave me full access to his father's large collection of local photographs. Chris and Maurice Lomas loaned me books and provided invaluable photos, while Paul Bowden was a great help with regard to Sitch House.

My friend David Hartley was a most informative companion on walks all over the area. Together we have explored overgrown cloughs, graveyards and ruins. He was the photographer. He also shared his own large stock with me. His wife, Lynne, and his mother-in-law, Jean Jackson, once cook at the Botany and at Taxal Lodge, have always afforded help and hospitality.

My computing skills are rudimentary. During our covid detention my wife Alison painstakingly tidied up my chaotic spacing and simplified my English. My sincerest thanks are due to my German friends Stefan Berger and Ansgar von der Osten, two lovers of the

Peak District, for their helpful comments.

Finally, I am especially grateful to Nye and Sue Rowlands for having put the same confidence in me as they did in my dad and his three little books. I hope any profit this book makes will help Footsteps in its great work for the community.

I am old enough to know that errors will inevitably have crept in. They are mine alone. As my dad always said: "Be merciful".

David Jackson

Cardiff 2021

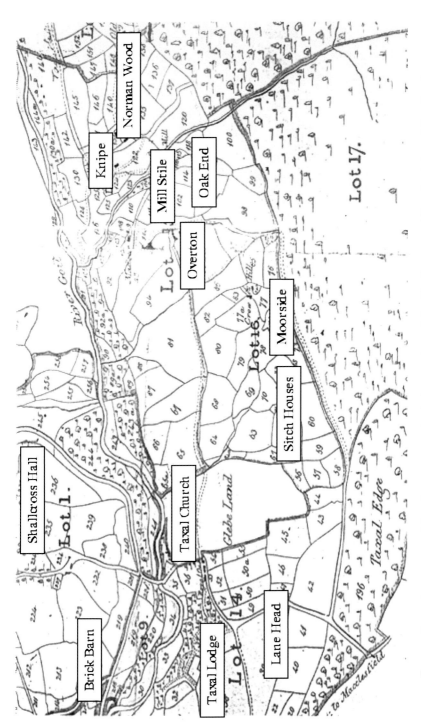

Extract from the map used for the attempted sale by auction of the Shallcross and Taxal estates at the Ram's Head, Disley, in 1832

Norman Wood

Knipe

Mill Stile

Oak End

Overton

Moorside

Sitch Houses

Shallcross Hall

Taxal Church

Brick Barn

Taxal Lodge

Lane Head

Lot 17.

Introduction

I owe everything to my parents. In the case of this book my debt, however, is to my father. But for him it would never have been possible even to contemplate writing it.

My mother was an "economic migrant" from Cumberland. My father, in contrast, was firmly rooted in the small Cheshire village of Kettleshulme. From 1912 to 1941 he lived with his parents, two brothers and two sisters in a warm, if for our taste today, over-crowded family nest. Bar several years away during the war and the final four months of his life, he spent the rest of his life less than two miles away, just over the Derbyshire border, in Whaley Bridge - all of it in four houses no more than 200 yards apart on Macclesfield Road.

After the war, despite working seven days a week in the mechanics' shop at the Botany Bleach Works at the bottom of Macclesfield Road, he managed to squeeze in as many walks as possible round the area with my mother and me. A mine of information about the places and people we encountered, he loved to pass on this knowledge - lightly and often with a chuckle, as he recounted some humorous tale or other. He seemed to me to know everyone we stopped to chat to. Not that that was surprising. As a joiner at E. A. Beard's in Wharf Road he had worked in the 1920s and 1930s all over the area: on Taxal Lodge, Colonel Ramsden-Jodrell's residence, on banks, farms and many of the large, older houses. Their owners seemed to have talked to him about much more than the work in hand. As a member of the football team in the 1930s, secretary of the local branch of the Woodworkers' Union, treasurer of the Oddfellows in Kettleshulme, and a steward at the Methodist Chapel in Whaley Bridge, he had over the years built up a wide circle of friends and acquaintances. His keen interest in people and places was allied to a phenomenal memory, which meant that he easily assimilated information and effortless ly retained it. A "gossip" of the kindly sort, quite without malice, he was also a good listener in whom people confided.

Once he had retired in 1977, he began keeping a diary and writing up his life history in an old Woodworkers' Union ledger. From that he progressed to writing short pieces for both the Anglican and Methodist magazines. Left a widower in 1991, he was encouraged to make them into a book by Nye Rowlands. *Arthur Jackson Remembers* appeared in 1998. To his surprise the first edition rapidly sold out. It gave him even greater satisfaction that the book raised a tidy sum for the local charity, Daniel's Light. He went on to write two more books, *Arthur Jackson Remembers More* (2000) and *The Life and Times of Arthur Jackson*, which came out in 2005 when he was 93. In the weeks before he died in 2011 and despite his poor sight and unsteady hand, he still laboriously wrote out a piece about a long dead Whaley Bridge stationmaster and gave it to his son whom he had just met here at the local Methodist Church. He had no intention of making that piece his last.

Right down to the last few years of his life, High Peak weather permitting, we would, on my regular visits, toil up to the top of Macclesfield Road, turn along the Linglongs and walk to Taxal. There his great-grandfather, Henry Morten, had kept the former Royal Oak. There, too, his grandmother had been lady's maid at the vicarage.

We often made a little pilgrimage down to the churchyard and struggled with the lines on the tombstone of Henry and his first wife Elizabeth, who had died, aged 43, having borne him ten children. In the lower section, at the corner by the gate, we would decipher once more the mossy lettering on his maternal grand-parents' upright head stone, which seemed to me perilously close to the haunches of the donkeys employed to keep the grass down. Further down, overgrown with brambles, was his paternal grandparents' grave.

Among the other headstones frequently visited were the distinctive headstone of a Kettleshulme Oddfellow, George Boothby, that of the pugilistic vicar, the Rev Samuel Evans, who had married my grandparents, and the graves of the Halls, the owners of the Botany Bleach Works, where my father worked. He brought their silent occupants to life again.

Although university research in Switzlerland and Germany, and then my job as a lecturer in Cardiff took me away, I always loved coming back to Whaley Bridge. As my grandmother reached the age of 87, still clear in her mind, if frail in her body, I had the good fortune to hear her tell - and re-tell! - her tales about Errwood, Taxal and Kettleshulme.

My father and I both knew that, one way or another, I would one day continue where he left off. Sadly, I left it too late and did not begin researching into the local past during his lifetime. He, for his part, never grew into the age of computers and Internet. Researching in large libraries and record offices was not part of his car-less world. Armed with the information to be found there, I could have helped him answer many of his unsolved questions. But unlike so many regretful sons and daughters I know, I was blessed, not simply with having heard his tales, but with knowing that he had committed so much information to paper and saved it from being forgotten for ever. In his nineties he once quietly confided that he hoped he would never be forgotten completely. I am truly glad that I always encouraged him, whatever his hesitations and doubts, never to stop writing. He never did.

Along the Linglongs, on the way to Taxal, just before the turn off to the right which takes you up to Taxal Edge, a gated driveway on the left leads down to Taxal Lodge. Now a vandalised shell, it served from the later 1950s to 2005 as a special school for boys from Stockport. Its gardens were still meticulously kept and once a year the public was granted access. My father had worked on the house in Colonel Ramsden-Jodrell's time, but he, like everyone else I ever asked, was unsure about the site's history. The existing building is clearly late Victorian/Edwardian in style, but what had stood there before, if anything? Had the Jodrells really lived here as well as at Yeardsley Hall throughout the centuries? Had the Taxal estate always belonged to them? The more I probed, the more my investigations brought to light a much more complex picture than I had ever imagined. A prominent "Blue Stocking" and even Horatio Nelson's mistress, Lady Hamilton, would figure in it.

Taxal Lodge in its heyday

Taxal Lodge today

The inn at one of the many stages in its long existence

A short step away from the Lodge is the former Royal Oak. My ancestors had been landlords there from the eighteenth century down to the 1920s. My grandmother told of a tragic event that had occurred before her time but had become part of Taxal lore: the discovery of the body of a newborn baby down by the Goyt and brought back to the inn. She also had tales of farmers "going on the spree". I was fairly sure I would find something about this and other goings on at the inn, at the church and on the farms in Taxal. I found more than I expected. The Royal Oak's fame even reached Irish newspapers.

I was determined to find more about my great-great-grandfather Moses Jackson and the reasons for him having been transported to Australia. My father thought it might have been for stealing a horse or a sheep. But he was only surmising. I hoped that, with the help of local newspapers from the time, and material relating to Moses's trial held at Chester Record Office, I could discover the truth. I did. His crime had nothing to do with horses or sheep.

Perhaps I could also discover the identity of the mysterious Kettleshulme man known as the "Earl of Rock Savage", about whom my father had been told and who, in some way unknown to him, was related to the Jacksons. Not surprisingly, the striking nickname had gripped my imagination as a boy and has never gone away.

My father always chuckled whenever he told me and other folk of the doings and sayings of another Kettleshulme "character", Jack Fidler, who, as a young man, had been a distinguished athlete. Perhaps old newspapers would yield details about his exploits. In actual fact I came across another Jackson, not one of "our lot", but one who, although not a Kettleshulme resident, had, as "Jackson of Kettleshulme", been a formidable runner in the 1840s. Researching his career took me into the chaotic, often extremely dodgy beginnings of modern athletics.

Kettleshulme school loomed large in my father's memories, and he had written more than once about his schooldays there. Equally important to him was the Library, renamed the Memorial Hall after the Great War. [He and his generation never referred to the First World War]. He had been its librarian for some years. Could I, I wondered, find more about its origins?

Since his youth he had also been a member of a friendly society, the Oddfellows, and had felt very honoured to be quoted and pictured in the volume published to mark its bicentenary in 2010. He often proudly reminded me that Moses Jackson had been one of the founder members of the Kettleshulme lodge. Late in his life, he entrusted to my safekeeping the treasured photo of his grandfather, taken when he was a delegate for the New Mills District at the Annual General Meeting in Cardiff in 1881. Perhaps there was something new to be unearthed about the society's early years.

If the school, the Library and the Oddfellows were so important to my dad, so, too, was the Wesleyan Chapel. Again I dared hope that I could find more information about its ministers and the big annual event, the chapel sermons. As it turned out, I was distracted from this by coming across a most unexpected "religious war" waged in local newspapers in 1870/71 one full of almost unbelievable incidents. It gradually emerged that one of the key combatants was the mysterious "Earl of Rock Savage". Having once rumbled his identity, I went on to discover the full extent of his insatiable appetite for feisty polemics of every sort and conducted under a variety of pen names.

One thing often leads to another. In this case what had started out as a search for Wesleyan ministers turned into an investigation into a charismatic Anglican curate who came to Kettleshulme in 1870 and produced a veritable religious revival in the village before moving on to Taxal. There he achieved something very similar; but it would be as the vicar of St Thomas's in Hazel Grove that he came into his own.

Spurred on by this discovery, I hunted for information on later Kettleshulme curates and vicars. To my great surprise, I came across a very different kettle of fish, a vicar dogged by debts, who had married a woman well "below his station". In my boyhood, on the way home from my grandparents, we used to walk along the narrow lane past the Old School and Ely Fold until we turned right onto the main road at a sharp, blind corner. My father would warn of cars approaching at speed and often reinforce his warning by telling of a woman who had been fatally injured near the spot. The worse for wear, she had been returning to the vicarage from the Swan. Was this the mysterious vicar's wife?

Various buildings had always prompted my questions as we walked round Whaley Bridge in the 1950s. On the way up to the cricket field, we passed a building which struck me as somewhat forlorn and deserted. As it was still known as the Drill Hall, it seemed logical to explore its links with the Territorials. Yet again a surprise lay in store for me. Initially the hall had had nothing to do with the military. In fact it was a product of one of the great movements in mid-Victorian England, the temperance movement, and had been built to house the Band of Hope.

My curiosity about the Territorials, once aroused, needed to be satisfied. It took me to their origins in the Rifle Volunteer Company founded in 1859. Just who had founded it and how had they tried to drum up support? Had they perhaps had their eye on the Band of Hope Hall from the outset?

The Mechanics' Institute in Market Street was another building that intrigued me as a boy. My grandfather, a saddler, had his workshop at the top of a steep flight of wooden stairs next to Carter's, the newsagent's, now Martin's.

From the windows I could look diagonally across at the heavy façade with its big clock and watch people either going up the steps and in at the main door or slipping down the side to the library in the basement. Who, I asked myself, had built it and why? Here, as with the Band of Hope Hall and the Rifle Volunteers, I soon became aware of just how close were the links some of Whaley Bridge's new, enterprising residents had had in mid-Victorian times with prominent figures and movements in Lancashire and Cheshire. The fear of revolutions and radical disturbances had, I also soon found, never been totally exorcised. My investigations into the Band of Hope and the Mechanics' Institute confronted me with another Jackson, Robert Jackson, again not one of "our lot". The more I delved into his career, the more he grew on me. His was a truly Victorian career with its steady rise and quite unexpected plunge into disgrace.

My granddad's workshop was above the *Evening News* sign

Vegetarianism - a rarity in a village where those who could afford it, like those who couldn't, were all proud of their roast beef. It turned out that, for a number of years, Whaley Bridge had been a veritable Mecca for prominent vegetarians. There had even been an Anti-Tobacco Society.

My mother was a strict teetotaller and had me sign the pledge at a tender age. Not surprisingly I was both terrified of and fascinated by public houses. (They were never accorded the more cosy sounding name of "pub"; they were far too dangerous for that!) I was whisked past the now closed White Horse at the bottom of Macclesfield Road. The Jodrell Arms, as its name indicated, was the grandest of the Whaley Bridge pubs and the one where my father's football team proudly celebrated its successes in 1938. Personally I was more taken by the White Hart, the old inn standing by the bridge over the Goyt. The decision to explore its past proved a good move. I grew quite fond of a publican, George Bowers, who, in the 1870s, manfully sought to keep abreast of the changing times, but sadly failed.

A late-Victorian photo of the White Horse. George Pearson is the licensee and the float represents the Chilcot Gunpowder Works at Fernilee

The White Hart

The knowledge that all these stories were there to be told and that I could perhaps fill in so many frustrating gaps motivated me to press on whatever the difficulties. Covid and with it enforced exile in Wales were just additional obstacles. What kept me going was the feeling that, despite ranging across disparate subjects, these stories did in many ways complement each other. Certain concerns kept re-surfacing. Gradually a picture of Victorian times crystallised.

The more the material expanded, the more it seemed sensible not to overload one book but instead divide it into three parts, with one booklet devoted to Taxal, one to Kettleshulme, and one to Whaley Bridge.

Hopefully the three will afford an interesting glimpse of a world which, despite being so far away and in many ways so different from ours has, nevertheless, left many visible traces that one can still see and enjoy today as one walks round the area.

Chapter 1

The unsung owners of Taxal Lodge

Like most schoolchildren in Whaley Bridge, I grew up thinking that the Jodrell family had been the leading family in Taxal from medieval times right down to the Second World War and beyond. We were told how a Jauderell had fought as an archer at the battle of Crecy in 1346 and another at Agincourt in 1415. The family had lived at Yeardsley Hall but moved at some stage from there to Taxal Lodge. This residence had been replaced early in the twentieth-century by the present building.

I can also remember being shown memorial inscriptions to the Jodrells inside Taxal church. If all that was not enough, the then grandest pub in Whaley Bridge, the Jodrell Arms, seemed to embody in stone this supposed centuries-old dominance.

Much less attention was paid to the Downes family. But there I was lucky: my grandmother, who had lived at Oakenend and Sitch House until she got married, grew up with tales of their doings. She told how, in the seventeenth century, one of them - Reginald Downes - had lived at neighbouring Overton Hall and each year confirmed his claim to his estate by blowing his horn on Windgather Rocks on Midsummer's Day. He held his court at the Hall, and had offenders hanged in the Gallows Yard beside it.

But it was not at all clear where the Downes family fitted into the Taxal story. What was also very confusing when I later read about Taxal, was that the monumental histories of Cheshire written by Ormerod and Earwaker confidently stated that Overton Hall had been pulled down early in the nineteenth century and another building known as Taxal Lodge built on the same spot. It had been taken down in 1835. This did not square at all with the situation with which I was familiar. Overton Hall had been replaced by the present-day farm and, for a long time, had the date 1810 above the door, whereas the building that I and everyone else knew as Taxal Lodge definitely stood on a quite different site further down the valley.

Overton Farm today

There was an additional perplexing complication. I knew that another family, the Shallcrosses, had lived for centuries just over the Goyt on the Derbyshire side. What had become of them? How had it come about that at the end of the nineteenth century Shallcross Hall was one of the residences of Sir Edward Cotton-Jodrell?

Shallcross Hall

It was all, to say the least, very confusing.

When, for the purposes of this project, I looked into all this more closely, I discovered to my surprise that, with regard to Taxal, the Jodrells were relatively late arrivals on the scene. On the other hand, male members of the Downes family had, from at least the thirteenth century, held the manor of Tackeshalch "by Forestry", i.e. as foresters of the king. As advowees or patrons of Taxal Church, they also enjoyed the right to present to the Bishop of Chester the clergyman appointed as parish priest. The manor remained in their hands until 1691, when the Reginald Downes, who figured in my grandmother's tales, sold the manor to his neighbour across the Goyt, John Shallcross of Shallcross, High Sheriff of Derbyshire in 1686 and 1710. In 1733 he sold it to John Dickenson, a Manchester merchant.

Five years before that he had already sold the Shallcross estate to Roger Jacson, MB (Bachelor of Medicine), who had married his middle daughter, Frances. As they were childless, the estate then passed to Roger's nephew, the Rev Simon Jacson who, in 1749, had married his cousin Anne, the daughter of John Shallcross's eldest daughter Margaret. Complicated as these marriage and inheritance arrangements were, they did explain why nobody with the name of Shallcross later figured in connection with the estate.

But it still did not explain how Sir Edward Cotton-Jodrell had come to have Shallcross Hall as one of his residences.

I did now know that another family called Dickenson had played a role in Taxal's history. Were there perhaps other families who had played a role too? Had there perhaps been a reason why a building known as Taxal Lodge had been demolished in the 1830s and not replaced until after 1900?

Chapter Two
Merchant invaders:

Hosting Bonnie Prince Charlie

From humble beginnings as weavers in Deansgate, Manchester, the Dickensons had risen to become wealthy linen and textile merchants. They provided the town with a succession of borough reeves — the elected official in charge of law and order. John Dickenson (1689-1769) was one from 1740 to 1750. His mother came from another wealthy Manchester family, the Birchs. Such was his wealth that although in 1743 Humphrey Birch had sold the Birch Estate in Rusholme to George Croxton, Dickenson was wealthy enough to buy it back two years later. However, his imposing town house in Market Street Lane continued to be his principal dwelling.

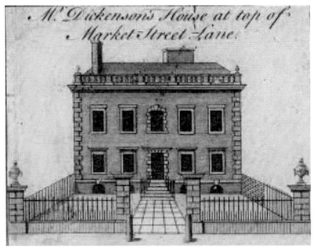

John Dickenson's House

The family is said to have earlier been Roman Catholic, and as Dickenson was a Jacobite and supporter of high church Anglicanism, it comes as no surprise that his palatial dwelling was chosen as a fitting residence for the Young Pretender, Bonnie Prince Charlie, when he and his army marched into Manchester in 1745.

Crowds flocked to greet him in front of the house. The family was supposedly so proud of the bed which Bonnie Prince Charlie slept on that it was taken to Birch Hall and kept there for many years. Somewhat surprisingly Dickenson does not seem to have suffered any negative consequences for having supportedthe failed rebellion. Later the house in Market Street Lane morphed successively into the Palace, the Palace Inn and the Palace Buildings.

Today the Arndale shopping centre occupies the site.

Lime kilns at Buxton

What motivated Dickenson to buy the Taxal Estate in 1733 - by which time the advowson had been separated from it? As a shrewd businessman, he would have been well aware of the opportunities its location afforded. Taxal was close to the Buxton area with its limestone,and there was a great market for lime, not only because of its importance in building work and road-making but also as a means of sweetening acidic common land that was being increasingly enclosed and brought into cultivation. In 1738 Dickenson took the plunge and bought four lime kilns on Grin Low, a hill overlooking Buxton.[1]

Remains of a lime kiln at Buxton

As there was as yet no railway running from the Buxton area to Whaley Bridge, and no canal system there to transport goods onwards, the lime – vast quantities of it - had to be hauled north and also across into Cheshire in horse-drawn carts.

Trunk roads

Dickenson's son, another John (1726-1810), an extremely hard-nosed businessman, continued the business. In his case we are fortunate that the letters he wrote to Richard Orford, steward for Peter Legh of Lyme Hall, Disley, make it possible to form a good idea of his activities and concerns in relation to Taxal.[2]

The course of the trunk road from Whaley Bridge to Buxton was understandably of great interest to him because of his lime kilns at Buxton. He, therefore, joined the committee of trustees charged with its construction. In 1775 he insisted that it should be made of limestone and resisted the proposal made by John Metcalf, Blind Jack of Knaresborough, the engineer to whom the project had been entrusted.

Metcalf wanted it to be made of gritstone, a cheaper option. Dickenson feared that he wanted to take unfair advantage of them. His proposal, he wrote, showed him to be a dirty fellow: if he lacked two eyes, he made up for it in other respects. Others, fearful of the cost, argued for an even cheaper option which in, Dickenson's opinion, would have produced a road of mud and dirt that it would be impossible to maintain.

Blind Jack

Dickenson was keen that the road from Horridge (i.e. Horwich End) to the Rev Jacson's coal pits at Shallcross should run in a pretty straight line below the land of another local landowner, "old Longden". This route,which he was ready to admit, did pose some problems, was in his interest. He did not get his way. The road swings away from the Goyt and describes a large loop up to

Extract from an 1830 map of the Jodrell estates. At the top it shows the newly-constructed Cromford & High Peak Railway running below the old road to Buxton.

The toll bar at Fernilee

Fernilee.

Dickenson's frustration with the project grew, and in 1777 he wrote to Orford that he had had so much trouble with the road that he wished to leave the committee.

Another trunk road, that between Macclesfield and Chapel-en-le-Frith, built in 1770, also greatly concerned him. He was not at all enthusiastic about the idea of erecting a toll bar at Horwich End.

With his usual tendency to indulge in self-righteous exaggeration he wrote to Orford on 26 February 1788 that "there was not a man in the kingdom who would go to greater lengths than he to serve the public and bear a share of the expense; but such a bar went against every principle of honour and justice, and he, as a man of honour, had to oppose it. Whereas the road had greatly profited the inhabitants of Kettleshulme and Rainow, nobody in Taxal had received the least benefit from it. If a bar were erected in Horridge, that would mean having to pay another toll in Whaley Bridge after a mere two-minute ride." Always one to pile on the agony, he claimed that nobody in the township had any more business to do with Macclesfield than if it were a town in Cornwall, and no team of horses had ever made the journey. His verdict: "I wish indeed the Road had never been made." Despite his objections a toll bar was eventually erected at the bottom of Macclesfield Road.

Taking on a man of God

But these concerns were as nothing compared with one revolving round mining matters. It positively obsessed him from the late 1770s, when he locked horns with his neighbour on the Derbyshire side of the Goyt, the already mentioned Simon Jacson. Jacson was anything but an otherworldly cleric. He followed the example of his uncle, Roger Jackson, who had already invested in mining at Shallcross. Dickenson claimed on 7 November 1781 that neither man, for upwards of 40 years, could have sold a single basket of fire coal without his assistance.

The source of the tension between the two men dated from 1768, when Jacson erected a wheel on land adjoining Dickenson's for the purpose of "laying dry and working" his coal mine. He continued to discharge the tailwater [slurry waste] onto Dickenson's land with out paying any "consideration". Finding that the wheel did not serve its purpose, he enquired as to whether he could erect one on Dickenson's land. Dickenson agreed. Furthermore, at his own expense - as he was always careful to stress - he had a tunnel constructed which protected Jacson's property. He trusted that this privilege would be rewarded with some handsome present, especially as, at the time, April 1785, he was, he claimed, in a distressed situation, having to support his family on an income of a mere £70 [something over £6,000 in 2017 terms]. He had looked upon Jacson as a man of noble and generous principles, and a few guineas would have done him an infinite service. No present had ever materialised.

In 1778 relations rapidly deteriorated even more when Dickenson toyed with the idea of going into coalmining himself. Fearing that the present informal agreement could obstruct his plans, he wanted it replaced by a formal one. The two parties agreed to go to arbitration and each appointed a representative. With Richard Orford acting as umpire, an agreement was reached. Dickenson's understanding of it was that Jacson would pay him a "trifling acknowledgement" of two guineas a year for use of the wheel, three, if he erected another, and £35 compensation for the tunnel.[3] But for him the key element in the agreement had always been that it should contain a clause stipulating that this arrangement could be terminated if he found it in any way obstructed his own work. So confident was he that this was what had been agreed and such was his trust in Orford that he did not read the final document before signing it. When he did, he was outraged to discover that Jacson had had clauses inserted which gave him extensive privileges for an unlimited time. Dickenson vented his indignation repeatedly in self-righteous rants.

They capture well the social tensions often existing between self-made business men, on the one hand, and the old landed gentry and clergy, on the other. Thus he sarcastically describes Jacson as this great gentleman who had never performed one benevolent action and had taken advantage of a man ignorant and unacquainted in such dark affairs [i.e. coalmining]. It was, he railed, not important whether a man had the education of a proud gentleman nor whether he was proud and arrogant, as too many of the clergy were, but rather what his actions showed him to be.[4] He, Dickenson, had enabled a man who had hindered every other neighbour from getting their own coal, open two collieries and line his pockets with thousands. Yet he had been treated most cruelly and barbarously, led like a lamb to the slaughter. He was now obnoxious to his "babes", his own flesh and blood; his wife was distraught, and his son John had told him to his face that he had injured him. As soon as public affairs mended, he would sell off every foot of land he had in the township. Despite all the bluster he stayed. He did, however, abandon his colliery scheme. He left Taxal for the last time on 11 February 1789 and spent the rest of his days at Birch Hall.

A "blue stocking"

Little of what his son John did at Taxal would make his stay noteworthy but for the fact that he brought an unusual bride with him.

On a visit to cousins in Northampton, John's mother, Sarah, had got to know Mary, the daughter of the Hon. Charles Hamilton.[5] The two struck up a life-long friendship. Sarah commended Mary for devoting her time to improving her mind and not wasting her time on "the childish dissipations so natural to her sex and age". At the same time she warned her that men wanted no rivals in knowledge and got angry with women who attained it. When John was sent to boarding school in Northampton, the two teenagers became close friends. In a letter of 13 August 1769 Sarah described to Mary the house in Taxal: it had a good view and, behind it, a grass plot from where woods, cottages, sheep and a rivulet [the Goyt!] could be seen.[6] More than that was not forthcoming. She believed that Mary would delight in drawing the view from it. Taxal, she added, was, damper than Northampton.

Mary's life changed dramatically when she was invited to become one of the governesses of the royal princesses at the court of George III and Queen Charlotte. Noticing that John Dickenson's letters to her had begun to turn into love letters, she felt it wise to discontinue their correspondence, but continued to correspond with his mother. The Crown Prince, infatuated with Mary, bombarded her with letters and presents.

Mary Hamilton

Although or perhaps because she resisted his advances, his passion burned bright until he found a woman more liberal with her favours, a married actress, Mrs Richardson. His final letter to Mary telling of his new passion ends: "PS Adieu. Adieu, toujours chère, oh Mrs Robinson!"

Increasingly finding court life monotonous and exhausting. Mary compensated for this by associating with a group of female intellectuals known as the Blue Stockings. It included Hannah More, Frances Burney, Mary Delany, and Eva Maria Garrick. In 1780 John, still in love with her, proposed. Her uncle, Lord Napier, had grave misgivings. He enquired about John's political principles and feared that his income would be inadequate even if his father gave him half of his. Mary turned John down. After the queen had finally allowed her to quit her post, she continued to live in London. John had not given up hope. In 1784 she received a letter from him saying he had come to London to see her.

She received him at six in the evening. The next day he proposed again.This time she accepted him. Given the short space of time intervening, the decision must have been hers and hers alone. In a social class where arranged marriages were the norm, it was a bold and brave independent decision. The marriage does also illustrate how the sons and daughters of wealthy self-made business men were being assimilated into the gentry and aristocracy.

Brass and blood were becoming bed fellows. This growing closeness partly explains why the UK did not witness a revolution like that which broke out in France five years later.

One might have expected John's father to have felt his family honoured by such a match, but he, like Lord Napier, had his own class-based misgivings. He feared that John might be marrying into a society more fashionable and extravagant than his own, and that Mary would disappoint his son's expectations of happiness. Fully aware of these sentiments, Mary wrote to her fiancé on 4 February 1784 to say that, had his father known that she had stayed in bed till ten o'clock reading, he would have exclaimed: "a fine London Lady this!" One can just imagine this industrious, no-nonsense businessman saying it in a pronounced Manchester accent!

Love prevailed and the two were married in London in 1785. They set up house at Taxal. Far from waxing lyrical about the new home that awaited her, John had written to Mary on 11 January 1775 to tell her that there was often a great deal of good company in Buxton. One could spend a few weeks there agreeably when the weather was good.[7] It is plain that Taxal itself was of little interest to him.

As he had promised, John helped Mary maintain her many contacts. As a result they were often away in the south. A daughter Louisa, born at Bath in 1787, was later christened at Taxal Church. Mary looked after all money matters, stressing to her father-in-law that they lived within their means, that she liked to produce a surplus at the end of the year and that they paid ready money for every article they bought. No doubt impressed by this, John senior grew fond of her and doted on his granddaughter, giving her four guineas towards a pony and, in 1794, 2/6 a week pocket money [about £10 in today's terms].

Two visitors

In June 1791 two visitors rolled up at the Lodge in their carriage. Amy Lyon, the daughter of a Cheshire blacksmith, a beautiful, enterprising girl, had gone to London, changed her name to Emily/Emma Hart, and for a time been Mrs Robinson's maid.

Portrait of Emma Hart painted by George Romney in 1785

She made the most of her charms, allegedly dancing nude on a table at an aristocratic stag party, before becoming the painter George Romsey's model and muse and the mistress of various grandees. One of them, Charles Greville, eager to get her out of the way for a while so that he could make a suitable marriage, steered her into the orbit of Sir Frederick Hamilton, a lonely elderly widower who was royal envoy at the court in Naples. Initially piqued, she soon saw that she could exploit this golden opportunity and joined Sir Frederick in Naples. Making the most of her modelling and acting talent, Emma became famous for her "attitudes" or "tableaux vivants", in which she portrayed classical figures and scenes. The audience had to guess their identity. The great German poet Goethe was among those who admired her performances. In June 1791 the couple visited Taxal. Sir Frederick insisted on preserving the fiction that they were not living together and had to be given separate rooms. One wonders what they made of Taxal. It was hardly Naples and Taxal Lodge was scarcely an Italian palace. Nor could Emma put on a show to mesmerize the Dickensons' tenants. Did they attend divine service at Taxal Church? Did they visit the Royal Oak? One thing is certain: given the difference in age between the two, tongues would have wagged busily. The couple eventually marriedin September 1791. She was 26, he was 60.

Lady Hamilton met Horatio Nelson in Naples in September 1793, but it was not until years later that the affair developed. Sir Frederick as a man of his time took the relationship in his elderly stride. Emma gave birth to Nelson's daughter, Horatia, in 1801.

The Prince Regent who had, as a youth been infatuated with Mary Hamilton, aroused Nelson's jealousy by transferring his infatuation to Emma. Helpful in all matters, Sir Frederick confidently reassured him that he need not worry: she was faithful to him! One wonders what John senior made of all this. One development in the family certainly did not meet with his approval. One of his daughters, Elizabeth, had fallen in love with an Italian, the Chevalier Palombo. John jun. was flattered by this. His father definitely was not. When his son tried to broach the topic with him, he took his stick and stomped out at the door:

> I cannot get my father to speak to me on the subject, not possessing much sensibility himself, he cannot imagine how cruelly he acts in trifling with others' money is unfortunately of too precious a quality in my father's eyes and, between ourselves, to a rich Jew or Jewess he would have married us all. He has avoided my looks all day and to prevent my speaking to him he has been poring his eyes out over a book of some sort."

The socialite and village life

John jun, while - diplomatically? - showing some interest in collieries, certainly did not inherit his father's passion for business. Nor did he show any interest in developing the Taxal estate. His interests lay elsewhere. A great socialite and avid party-goer, he revelled in name-dropping and court and high society gossip, flitting continually between Buxton, Bath, Cheltenham, and London. His letters to his wife may demonstrate how devoted he was to her but, in terms of their content, they are best described as the tittle-tattle of a court correspondent. Very little in them has anything to do with Taxal. One can only hope that Mary's letters to him, once they have been digitised, may be more informative. One letter did catch my attention. Written on 10 December 1790 in Buxton, where he was taking the waters for his aches and pains and hobnobbing with gentlefolk, it reads: "I forgot to order the Taylors to provide for the tenants' dinner on Tuesday next. In case I cannot return by that day I would not have them disappointed. Let them dine comfortably together and pay their rents when I come home" [8] Edward Taylor was mine host at the Royal Oak. One of his daughters, Louisa, married James Collier. One of their daughters, Betty, married my great-great-grandfather Henry Morten, who, in his turn, became publican at the Royal Oak. Like Taylor he, too, put on the half-yearly audit dinners for the tenants on the estate.

John Dickenson had little in common with his tenants. They lived in a different world. One cannot imagine him enjoying a drink and chat with them at the Royal Oak. He shows no Rousseaustic interest in supposed unspoilt children of nature nor any romantic love of nature itself. He was no Wordsworth going for a ramble up to Windgather Rocks or writing poems enthusing about the Goyt Valley or Taxal's moors. But equally there is also nothing to indicate that, although he had acquired his licence to hunt game, he was interested in aping the aristocracy by spending a great deal of time hunting and shooting and then having his team of gamekeepers neatly lay out huge hauls of game for all to admire.

As yet there is nothing to indicate that Mary herself paid much attention to local folk or was interested, as was her sister-in-law, Sarah, in the changes being wrought in the north west by industrialisation. It would be marvellous if it turns out that she wrote to her absent husband about village life in Taxal and Whaley Bridge or about the condition of women in the area. One hopes, too, that her letters may say something revolutionary about the events in

1789. It was only a matter of time before the couple left Taxal. In 1793 the estate was sold and they moved in succession to Birch Hall, Bath and London. In 1797 they bought Leighton Hall in Leighton Buzzard, an altogether grander building than Taxal Lodge.

In 1811 they moved again, this time to London. In 1815 their only child, Louisa, married General Sir William Anson. Mary died in 1816, John in 1842. Their stay in Taxal had been but a brief interlude.

A new family comes onto the scene, the Bowers.

The Dickensons in1797

Notes

1. See John Leach, "Grin Hill, Buxton, a major Derbyshire limestone quarry", in *Derbyshire Archaeological Journal*, vol. 116(1996), and John Leach, *The Book of Buxton*, Barracuda Books, 1987.

2. The following section relies on the collection *A corpus of late-eighteenth century letters*, edited by Linda van Bergen and David Denison. The letters are held by the John Rylands Library in Manchster, to whom I am grateful for being allowed to make use of them. See humanities.manchester.ac.uk/medialibrary/files/daviddenison/orford/1htm

3. Letter to Richard Orford 3.8.80

4. Letter to Richard Orford, 18.8.80

5. This material is taken from *Mary Hamilton, afterwards Mrs John Dickenson at court and at home.From letters and diaries*, ed. byEliza beth and Florence Anson, London 1925

6. HAM 3/1/1, Mary Hamilton Papers, Archives Hub, Manchester University, archiveshub.jisc.ac.uk, Manchester University, UK.

7. HAM 3/1/6

8. HAM 1/2/3.

Chapter Three
Two brothers

Miles Bower, born around 1661 in Sedburgh, found his way from there to Manchester. The Bowers prospered. Miles (1696-1780) and his son Miles (1722-1756), were among the most prominent hatters in Manchester and both occupied important civic posts. In 1744 Miles jun. married Sarah Marsden, the daughter of a wealthy Chester merchant. Such was his stature in Manchester that he was invited to lay the first stone of the Infirmary in 1753 and became Manchester's chief constable. He died in February 1756 at his house in Cupid's Alley, Deansgate, later renamed Atkinson Street after the man who took over the Bowers' factory.

Two of his sons, Foster and John, become part of the Taxal story. Foster, the younger of the two, was baptised on 30 May 1748 at St Ann's. After attending Manchester Grammar School, he went up to Oxford at the age of 15 to study law. Enjoying the patronage of Sir Joseph Yates, he rapidly became one of the highest paid lawyers in the land, earning between £3,000 and £4,000 per annum. In 1780 that represented between £260,000 and £345,000 in 2017 terms. Foster progressed from being head of the Oxford Circuit to becoming recorder of Chester in 1788. In 1793 he bought the manor of Taxal and the Overton Estate from John Dickenson, and in the following year the Shallcross Estate from Dickenson senior's great bugbear, the Rev Simon Jacson.

Grand designs

What motivated this wealthy bachelor in his early forties to acquire a country residence at Taxal? Did he want, when time allowed, to get away from London and Chester, in order to be close to his brother John who had married Frances Jodrell of Yeardsley and Twemlow in 1775 and changed his name to Bower-Jodrell? (This stipulated name change always ensured that when there was no male Jodrell to carry on the line, the family's name never died out. A Cotton became a Cotton-Jodrell, a Ramsden, a Ramsden-Jodrell!) If this was Foster's hope, he had miscalculated badly. In 1779 John had bought Henbury Hall near Macclesfield. Built in 1742 in the neo-classical style for Sir Peter Meredith, this fashionable mansion was certainly in a different league from Yeardsley Hall. Originally John had intended to extend and beautify his wife's ancestral home, but, presumably seduced by Henbury[1] and Cheshire life, he abandoned the scheme after having had part of the hall demolished. It became a farm, and the Jodrells absentee landowners and landlords.

The later Yeardsley Hall

Or was Foster Bower attracted by the striking position which the timber-framed Elizabethan lodge occupied high above the Goyt? He was well aware that, given his ample means, he could replace it with a splendid, fashionable building in the classical style - one that would match his brother's. He could also reach Taxal relatively easily from Chester now that the trunk road between Macclesfield and Chapel-en-le-Frith had greatly improved the rough and extremely hilly stretch between Hurdsfield and Kettleshulme. Manchester was well within reach, while fashionable Buxton was less than eight miles away. Nor was he blind to the estate's financial potential. Were he to establish plantations on the extensive moors, he would be guaranteed a healthy income from the sale of timber. No doubt he would also have been conscious that rents and extraction rights in connection with the coal workings at Shallcross promised solid returns, too.

Once his architect had come up with the design for the new house and gardens, the site was cleared. Builders, craftsmen, and gardeners set to with a will, while an expert in forestry matters presumably guided a team of labourers in laying out extensive larch and fir plantations on Hoo Moor, Ladbitch and Taxal Edge.

Foster Bower did not live to enjoy the fruits of their labours. He died, after a short illness, at his chambers in Lincoln's Inn in February 1795. He was only 45. [2]

What would become of Taxal now?

Notes

1   Henbury Hall was bought in 1957 by Sir Vincent de Ferranti, whose son had it demolished in the 1980s and replaced by a hall in the style of a Palladian, rotunda-shaped temple.

2   Unfortunately I have been so far unable to unearth any plan, drawing or paintings of the new lodge. Nor has, as far as I know, the lithograph been preserved that was later produced when it was put up for sale in 1832.

Chapter Four

The ignominious fate of Taxal Lodge

Foster Bower left the bulk of his property to his brother John. But his days, too, were numbered. He died the following year. The Yeardsley, Taxal and Shallcross estates all passed to his son, Francis. What was to be done with the two estates? It was not a propitious time to put them onto the market. The Land Tax figures for Taxal in 1796 show that the value of land and property had dropped. It was, however, urgent to sort out the future of Taxal Lodge if it was not to be a drain on finances and become a prime target for theft and vandalism. A tenant would have to be found.

On 23 February 1797, an advert, headed "Country House to Let", appeared in the *Derby Mercury*

> *Taxal Lodge in the County Palatinate of Chester, furnished or unfurnished, for five or three years, and to be entered upon immediately. Taxal Lodge is a new built stone house, very handsomely finished and beautifully situated, six miles from Buxton, eight miles from Macclesfield and ten from Stockport with garden, coach houses, stable, barn, shippons and other conveniences for a family and any quantity of good land not exceeding 40 statute acres.*
>
> *The house consists of a drawing room 27 feet by 18, Eating Room 30 feet by 21, Breakfast Room 24 feet by 18, and a Gentleman's Parlour 18 feet by 14, with very convenient offices on the first floor. Upstairs good bedchambers, with rooms for*

servants. NB a reasonable permission of sporting
on the manors of Taxal and Shallcross will be
granted to a tenant.

The first tenant was William Hodson, a Manchester merchant who had made his money as a chapman buying raw cotton or silk and then putting it out. A prominent figure in the town, he was one of the three church wardens and president of the Church and King Club, which met at the Bull's Head. Faced by the revolution which had broken out in France in 1789, its goal was to preserve constitutional order, liberty and property against levellers and republicans. Publicans were put under intense pressure not to allow any radicals to meet on their premises.[1] In 1790 the club commissioned a frosted silver medal with George III on it in order to commemorate the defeat of the attempt made by dissenters in the House of Commons to have the Test and Corporation Acts repealed. These acts required all public and civil servants, university professors, lawyers, etc. to be members of the Anglican church. Hodson was clearly a very conservative-minded gentleman.

High on the list of attractions Taxal Lodge afforded him was the prospect of enjoying the "sporting", i.e. the shooting. In 1798 he acquired the necessary game licence. But he did not stay long. Perhaps he fell on hard times. In 1799 a partnership between him and another Manchester merchant was dissolved. Whatever the reason, he gave up the tenancy in 1799.

On 3 September an advert appeared in the *Manchester Mercury*. A dog kennel had now been added; "cow houses" replaced "shippons", a term town dwellers might not be familiar with; the amount of land was increased to "a limit of 50 statute acres"; and the "gentleman's parlour" was replaced by "library". Also added were two kitchens, a housekeeper's room, a servants' hall, and a butler's pantry. The sporting facilities were elaborated on:

A tenant, if so desired, may be accommodated

*with the deputation of three extensive manors stocked
with hares, partridges and moor game, likewise with
any part of the furniture, farming stock, etc. at a fair
valuation.*

The Land Tax returns for 1800 show Frances Jodrell to be the owner and occupier, but by 1801 the occupant is C H Noel, Esq. Christopher Henry Noel was born at Wellingore Hall in Lincolnshire in 1774. His father, Christopher Nevile, the husband of a daughter of Baptist Noel, the 4th Duke of Gainsborough, was a Colonel in the South Battalion of the Lincolnshire Regiment. The Neviles are always described in histories of the peerage as one of the most powerful houses amongst the chivalry of England. Christopher Henry studied at Cambridge before joining the Rutland Fencible Cavalry, a body serving at home. He would rise to become its Lieutenant Colonel. In 1798 he changed his name to Noel. He was only at Taxal for a short time. What he did during his time there is a mystery. One imagines that, had he stayed, he would have relished the hunting and shooting.

He was succeeded in 1804 by Samuel Gratrix. Samuel and his brother Benjamin, calico printers and dyers of note, owned a warehouse in High Street, Hulme. In 1799 Samuel took out a patent on a new method of dying and staining colours on cotton and linen. In 1801 the *Annual Report of World Events* commended it as a great advance on the previously used method. The brothers founded a printworks at Furness Vale in 1794. It must have been extremely gratifying to Samuel's self-esteem to live at such a splendid residence as Taxal Lodge. He could not get much closer than this to leading the life of a true country gentleman. Taxal was also highly convenient, being only a few miles from his works. He acquired a game certificate and presumably enjoyed the shooting. He was still there in 1810 but gone by 1812. Was he, one wonders, already feeling the financial pressures which led to bankruptcy proceedings being brought against the company in 1821? In 1815 he is reported as living at Furness Lodge. One wonders if this was the "capital messuage or dwelling house" featuring in the notice of the sale of the printworks in 1855. [2]

A William Hyne was the tenant in 1813. He was followed in 1814 by George William Newton. Newton proved to be a long-term tenant, and an interesting one.

The squire of Aspenshaw

Around 1700 another Bower family, recognising the potential of the Torrs area in New Mills, opened a fulling mill, paper mill and tanning yard there.[3] A member of the family, George Bower, later married into the Buckley family, who lived at Aspenshaw Hall in Thornsett.

Aspenshaw Hall today

George William, their second son, was born in 1788. When George's grandfather died in 1803, his mother inherited the Ollersett estate and built Ollersett Hall.[4] George and his wife took up residence at Taxal Lodge. Reputedly a popular local magistrate and country gentleman, he was a keen member of the Loyal Wellington Club in Stockport, becoming its chairman.[5] Its name indicates its staunchly Tory character. Radicals, republicans and revolutionaries were the enemy. The couple moved in the highest county circles, and a card has been preserved which shows his wife as a patroness of a grand fancy-dress charity ball held in 1828 for the benefit of the Stockport Dispensary and House of Recovery, later to be known as Stockport Infirmary.

In Taxal George William also rented Overton Farm and Lane Head Farm. Always intent on expanding and developing his landholdings, he may have dreamt of one day buying the whole of the Taxal estate.

Interested in forestry, as he was, he could have had his eye on the maturing plantations. Much later, in 1859, he would publish *A Treatise on the growth and future management of timber trees and other rural subjects.* He was also interested in "sporting" activities, and in his old age wrote a book *Rural sports and how to enjoy them.* Not that his interests ended there. He was also a keen member of the Manchester Agricultural Society, winning prizes for the best year-old stirk and bull in 1824.

As a magistrate Newton was involved in several notable cases. The first of them was the brutal murder in 1823 of William Wood, a murder commemorated by the so-called "Murder Stone" on the roadside between Stoneheads and Disley.

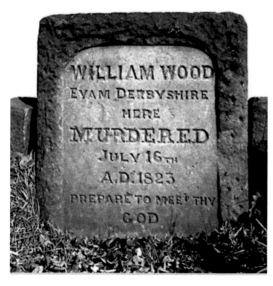

The Murder Stone

Joseph Dale, one of the three murderers, appeared before Newton at the Cock, later renamed the Jodrell Arms.[6] His experience during this case impelled him years later to provide evidence to the commissioners looking at ways of establishing an efficient constabulary. Their report appeared in 1839.

By that time Newton had long since come to the conclusion that local constables were incompetent. As an example of "the type of man village constables often are," he cited Mellor, the Whaley

Bridge constable who had taken Dale to Chester for the trial. Returning to his lodging, Mellor was told that the ostler there had been found dead in the privy. His reaction was simple: "Yes", he said "I saw him dead there three hours ago, but I have had trouble enough in finding one dead man. I'll be b...... if I ever find another." [7]

In 1826 Newton was involved in a case which was one of the great news stories of that year and the next, the abduction of a young heiress by Edward Gibbon Wakefield (1796 - 1852).

EDWARD GIBBON WAKEFIELD.
Founder of New Zealand.

Edward Gibbon Wakefield

In 1816, Wakefield, then aged 20, had abducted Eliza Pattle, a 16 year old ward in chancery and married her in Edinburgh. A silver-tongued individual, he had somehow convinced the Lord Chancellor and the girl's mother to recognise the marriage and had been awarded an extremely generous settlement. Four years later his wife died in childbirth. In 1826, in need of capital and connections if he were to realise his grand political ambitions, he hatched a similar scheme: he would abduct and marry a girl completely unknown to him, Ellen Turner, the fifteen-year-old daughter of William Turner of Pott Shrigley Hall. Turner was High Sheriff of Cheshire and owner of a calico printing and spinning works. With him as his father-in-law he could go places. The whole incredible tale of the abduction, which led in zigzag fashion from Liverpool to Gretna and then to France, would be splashed all over the newspapers in titillating detail. Unfortunately for Wakefield, this time his strategy failed. Ellen was reunited in Calais with her uncle and a warrant issued for Wakefield's arrest.[9] On 31 March his brother, William, appeared before Newton and Thomas Legh of Lyme at the Ram's Head in Disley, charged with being his accomplice. He was committed to Lancaster Castle.[10] Wakefield himself returned from France, rode to Taxal and handed himself in to Newton as the magistrate who had signed the warrant for his apprehension for a capital felony. Everything proceeded in a most gentlemanly fashion:

> *This event being quite unexpected by Mr Newton, the worthy magistrate requested him to remain at Taxal till Mr Turner's legal representatives could arrive, and accordingly Mr Wakefield slept at Taxal that night* [11]

After having been examined at the Ram's Head by Newton, S. P. Humphries and G. Tatton, Wakefield was committed to Lancaster Castle to be tried for a felony. At the Assizes he was sentenced to three years gaol in Newgate, his brother to three in Lancaster gaol. Wakefield made good use of his time in prison - writing about colonisation and the strategies to be adopted by the British government. Subsequently he master-minded the settlement of New Zealand and also played a key role in Canada and South Australia.

After the death in 1827 of his aunt, Frances Clare Bower, Newton inherited Aspenshaw, and three years later, on his mother's death, Ollersett. Although he moved in 1830 to Aspenshaw, he seems to have rented Taxal Lodge and the two farms for some time afterwards. But in his eagerness to acquire ever more land, he over-reached himself. In 1836, over four days, the furniture at Aspenshaw went under the hammer. The Newtons moved away; his wife died at Cheltenham in 1838; he himself returned to Ollersett late in life and died there in 1871, aged 83.

An auctioneer's hype

Newton's move to Aspenshaw was not welcome news for the Jodrells,who were again confronted with the problem of what to do with Taxal Lodge. Francis Bower-Jodrell had died in 1829, and ownership of the various estates passed to his son John William Jodrell. He and his advisers took the bull by the horns and decided to auction off the Shallcross and Taxal estates as one lot. To do this, they enlisted the London auctioneer, George Henry Robins, who was famed for conducting proceedings at the Great Piazza, Covent Garden, with a showman-like bravura.

George Robins

Robins was renowned for maximising the positive features of any property coming under his hammer, highlighting its potential, and transforming drawbacks into positive advantages. He was definitely the man to get the best possible price for the estates.

The notice of the auction appeared in a host of newspapers. On 16 April 1831 the *Macclesfield Courier* contained an appetizer. It announced the sale of very extensive freehold estates including several excellent farms: the residence of Taxal Lodge amid the beautiful scenery of Derbyshire, exclusive fishery to a considerable extent in the river Goit (sic), capital shooting over the moors, water, corn- and powder mills. The Buxton to Manchester turnpike road, it added, passed through the estate.

This notice was followed on 3 April by a much fuller one, announcing the auction of the estates as one lot at the Auction Mart near the Bank of England at twelve o'clock on 9 June.

The catalogue Robins produced is a match for the slickest and glossiest of brochures crafted by today's top London estate agents.

The hype begins at the very outset. Robins deals in superlatives. "The beautiful scenery" is ramped up to "the most beautiful scenery in Derbyshire". This verbal inflation sets the tone for all that follows. Robins's target is some wealthy merchant or manufacturer anxious to join the landed gentry but at the same embark on a sound, financially profitable venture rather than just fritter money away on a folly. He skilfully emphasises every possible advantage likely to appeal to this particular type of buyer. Thus, having emphasised that the Derbyshire estate, i.e. Shallcross, is entirely free of tithes and that the domain, including the fine moors, exceeds 4,500 acres, the advert immediately evokes the splendid business prospects. On offer is an inexhaustible supply of coals, "the pecuniary advantages from which are at present considerable." Future prospects are even better: "perspectively, on the termination of short leases, the income will be immense." To complete this particular seductive prospect, Robins adds: "A just discovered vein of coal promises benefits which are almost incalculable."

Having highlighted the pecuniary advantages the notice goes on:

> *Embosomed in its luxurious plantations, it has for*
> *many a long year been the subject of the passing*
> *traveller's praise and is accounted at Buxton one of*
> *the lions of the place and consequently frequented by*
> *all who pretend to good taste.*

One could hardly cram more attractions into a single sentence.

Pairing aesthetic beauty with practical gain, Robins transforms the Taxal section of the Goyt valley into a romantic rural paradise. Nobody is to imagine that the periodic flooding which, on several occasions during the course of the century, would severely damage both the bridge over the Goyt at the bottom of Church Brow and also installations serving the Botany Bleach Works, might constitute a drawback.

Damaged but repaired after a flood in 1872 this bridge had to be demolished after another flood in 1881

Its successor

On the contrary, the flooding of the large, flat meadow directly below the Lodge only makes it the most productive in the county:

The situation is really beautiful; it overlooks a luxuriant valley for several miles through which the river Goyt pursues its circuitous and irregular course, sometimes silently, although it must be admitted that sometimes its impetuosity has been irresistible and the consequence has been that by this sudden freak of nature the dry lands along its banks have at once assumed the refreshing appearance of water meadows, thus becoming influential in securing the heaviest crops in the county when a dry season had been less courteous to its neighbours."

Then it's back to other great financial opportunities afforded a buyer. "Those who have seen the plantations, scarcely need a comment on them. They extend upwards of one thousand acres, thriving and prosperous, and are considered the finest without exception in the county." Given that timber was in such demand for houses and barns, mine props, ships, barges, etc., the plantations set out by Foster Bower's labourers did indeed promise a good return, now that they were nearing maturity.

If that prospect was not enough to whet a potential buyer's appetite, perhaps mention of the stone quarries higher up the valley would:

They are very prolific and water carriage is close at hand [In plain English the canal barges at Whaley Bridge.] *Turnpike roads intersect the property and the famed railroad* [i.e. the High Peak and Cromford Railway], *which has long since began* (sic)*, most auspiciously progresses many miles through the territorial possessions [.....]. The time is not far away when the Manchester rail-road, being completed, will, by its rapid intercourse with the metropolis of London, give a considerably increased value to the estate."*

Members of the Canal Group doing their bit for the Basin

The Whaley Bridge-Manchester line would be completed in 1857. Had it existed in 1831, Robins would have had a field day. Without naming Pickford's transport business based at Goytsclough Quarry, he goes on: "The stone quarries contributed their full proportion to the most admired residences in Regent Street and the Park." The link between Taxal and elegant London is lodged subconsciously in the reader's mind. A buyer need not fear he is buying into some rough, unglamorous life-style.

Robins now judges it time to return to the alluring prospect of being able to indulge in activities that had always been the preserve of the aristocracy and landed gentry. The section "The Preserve for Game" pulls out all the stops: "These preserves are proverbially good. Grouse and black cock are in great abundance. The estate is famed for lots of woodcocks during the winter." But, once again mindful that a potential buyer might be deterred by the thought that all the ground could be rough moorland of poor agricultural quality, Robins judiciously adds: "Except for on the moors, the congeniality for agricultural pursuits of the soil has never been doubted. It has the great advantage of being generally of a convertible character." In other words it can be used either as arable land, meadow or pasture.

Knowing just how important it is to hammer home key points, Robins once again emphasises that the Derbyshire estate is entirely tithe free and now adds as a further inducement the information that the poor rates are exceedingly low. In other words, any self-made man priding himself on his industry, will not have to dip deep into his pocket in order to subsidise the feckless poor. Buxton, it is stressed, is close at hand and Manchester but a few short miles away..

> *The present low rental exceeds £2,300 a year* [circa £265,000 in 2017 terms] *and it may be safely assumed that with a view to a safe and permanent investment it cannot be surpassed, while at the same time it presents to a sporting gentleman inducements that it would be very difficult to resist."*

A buyer is guaranteed to get the best of all possible worlds.

Particulars, with plans lithographed and a sketch of Taxal Lodge with its Corinthian pillars, would be available twenty eight days prior to the sale.

The brochure is a truly virtuoso performance in seductive hype. Imagine the effect if Robins had been able to reinforce his text with glossy photos or provide a promotional video!

The notice was reinserted in the *Macclesfield Courier* several times and appeared in newspapers all over England. Perhaps because requests for the catalogue were slow in coming in, the date of the auction was shifted to 23 June. On 5 July the *Chester Courant* reported that it had gone ahead on the appointed date and that the estate had been sold for £66,950, which in 2017 terms amounts to some £4,540, 000. John William Jodrell and his advisers would, one imagines, have been well-pleased. Unfortunately for them the buyer must have subsequently pulled out. The estates remained unsold.

Flailing around

What were John William Jodrell and his advisers to do? They

decided to try to find a tenant. This time the shooting rights were made into the main attraction. A notice in the *Macclesfield Courier* announced that for any number of years, from May 12 next, Taxal Lodge, coach house, stable, barn, dog kennels, garden, pleasure gardens and any quantity of land to suit the convenience of the tenant, could be rented. Also included was the exclusive right of shooting over 4,500 acres, comprising the Taxal, Shallcross and Goyt's Head estates. They were, it went on, all well adapted for any description of game, particularly grouse and black cock, which were in great abundance. It was also a favourite resort for woodcocks in the winter season. The estates were to be held either together or separate, by private contract. The final inducement contained in the notice is that the shooting over the adjoining estates of Yeardsley and Disley, upwards of 1,500 statute acres, could be obtained if desired. Mr Firth, land agent in Macclesfield, would provide particulars.

But even this seductive offer found no takers. There was nothing for it but to split both estates into lots and try to auction them off individually. On 6 December the *Macclesfield Courier* announced that Mr Winstanley would conduct this auction at the Ram's Head, Disley, on Wednesday, 4 January 1832. The notice is couched in much less florid terms. Not that it is entirely free of hype. Thus it stresses that in a few years, when the timber reaches maturity, it will yield an "amazing" interest. On December 24 the newspapers carried details of the 28 lots. [12]

Even this move did not meet with any success. In the depressed 1830s merchants and mill-owners, flush with money and avid to get their hands on an investment estate in the country, were few and far between. In the cotton industry trade was bad.

The Taxal Lodge saga dragged on. On 28 July an advert appeared in the *Macclesfield Courier* under the headline" Shooting over 4,000 acres of land to be let". Taxal Lodge is now on offer together with the right of shooting over the estates of Taxal, Yeardsley,

Shallcross and Disley. Lying together, these afford "every facility for the preservation of game".

> *No part whatsoever of this property will now be sold. An incoming tenant may therefore be certain that no diminution of the manor will take place, to the injury of his shooting. Great terms, for not less than seven years, £200 per annum.*
> *Good references will be required.*

J H Beswick of Macclesfield, who had become land agent for the Jodrells, had a new advert drawn up. It focused on the Lodge and appeared in the *Manchester Times* on 26 October 1833:

> *This delightful residence is situate on an eminence, enclosed in the woods and plantations surrounding it, commanding a beautiful view of the woods, grounds, and the wood on the opposite side of the valley, as well as of the church which is contiguous and in which are two pews belonging to it.*

The measurements of the dining-room, drawing room, breakfast room and study are provided, the marble chimney pieces, entrance hall, and oak staircase highlighted. The first floor is described as having five bedrooms and a dressing room, the second five; there are a servants' hall, a housekeeper's room, a kitchen, a brewhouse, a dairy and larders, three bedrooms above, and the most excellent cellaring; the out-offices comprise a four-stalled stable, a two-stalled one, a loose stall, a harness room, three coach-houses with a loft over, a game-keeper's room, and dog kennels; the garden, yards and pleasure ground contain 14 acres 3 roods 2 perches. Rent is not so much an object as a respectable tenant.

Further particulars can be obtained on application from J.H. Beswick, land agent, Macclesfield, or Messrs Grimsditch, Hubbard and Welsh, solicitors, Macclesfield.

The notice, like all its predecessors, fell on stony ground.

Demolition

By the time Taxal Lodge reappeared in the *Macclesfield Courier* on 4 June 1836, a brutal decision had been taken - to have it demolished. The notice was addressed specifically to builders, directing their attention to valuable building material. This was to be sold by auction at the Cock Inn [later known as the Jodrell Arms], at six o'clock in the afternoon of the 13th. The materials at Taxal Lodge, the barn, coach house, walls and stable, were to be taken down by the purchaser. They were of the best description, consisting of a portico of pure stone, with two fronts of beautiful ashlar stone, good Westmoreland blue slate, oak, and good red deal flooring joists in good preservation, mahogany doors, marble chimney pots, grates and a great variety of other materials of a corresponding description.

This drastic throw of the dice did the trick. One wonders just how many builders, having inspected the valuable items on offer and secured them at the auction, subsequently rolled up at the Lodge, carefully dismantled the main building to get at their purchases, and, with equal care, loaded the items bought onto their horse-drawn carts and hauled them away. All the remaining structures must have been demolished and removed, too.

Estate Map of 1839 showing Taxal Lodge

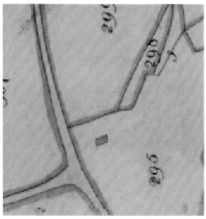

The Tithe map of 1844 shows only Taxal Lodge Cottages

When the Lodge was rebuilt in 1904, the drive was laid on the other side of the cottages.

One wonders what became of the materials carted away. What was incorporated into other buildings in the area? Did anything find its way to Errwood, where construction of an ambitious new hall was begun in the mid-1830s? But building fashions had changed by then and the Grimshaws were hardly in need of second-hand goods.

The site would remain unoccupied until Sir Edward Cotton-Jodrell, happy to have Shallcross Hall as one of his residences, had Taxal Lodge built in 1904 to accommodate his agent, T.C. Toler. Colonel Henry Ramsden, "owd Rammy", as he was known to the locals, married Cotton-Jodrell's daughter, Dorothy Lynch, in 1902, and the couple later made Taxal Lodge their residence.

Taxal Lodge is now a vandalised shell, its gardens a tangled wilderness.

Notes

1   See Archibald Prentice, *Historical sketches and personal recollections of Manchester*, London,1851

2   See Chris Bond, *The Life and Times of Furness Vale Printworks from 1794 to 1925*, Furness Vale History Society 2012, p. 57.

3   For information on Aspenshaw, the Bowers and Newtons see stevelewis.me.uk/p43.php, and Ron Weston, *Men of property the Bowers and Newtons,* New Mills Local History Society

4   See Ron Weston, *The Bowers and the Newton in New Mills*, New Mills History Notes N° 28, New Mills, 2000

5   *Manchester Courier 25.6.25*

6   *Manchester Mercury 6.8.23*

7   *First Report of the Commissioners appointed to Inquire as to the Best Means of Establishing an efficient constabulary force in the counties of England and Wales* London 1839, p. 105f.

8   See Abby Ashton and Audrey Jones, *The Shrigley Abduction,* Sutton Publishing Strand 2005

9   *Lancaster Gazette 8.4.1826* - among many!

10   *Chester Chronicle 16.5.1826*

11 *Liverpool Mercury 2.6.1826*

12   In some cases the occupants of farms and, houses are named, but by no mean all. Fortunately, in the 1960s, John Brocklehurst, a farmer, allowed William Eyre, the great local historian, to see a list he had of the properties and their occupants

Typed, on a sheet of lined A8 paper, It reads:

PARTICULARS OF SALE OF FREEHOLD PROPERTY JANUARY 1832

Shallcross Hall John Morten; Far End Farm John Morten , (in pencil: Elnor Lane Way); Folds George Bennett; Elnor Lane Head Robert

Bennett; Mill House Jonathan Jodress, (in pencil: beginning of Elnor Lane) This lot sold subject to the goit or feeder which conveys water to turn the wheels for pumping water from Shallcross colliery; the Folds Ellis Cooke; Shaw Stile John Beard; part of Shaw Stile (gunpowder mills) Messrs Williamson & Co; Over Hill William Bennett; Lee Head Phillip Ollerenshaw; Shallcross Mill John Higginbottom , the corn mill is well supplied with water which turns three pairs of stones and a dressing machine in pencil: at the beginning of Elnor Lane); Bennett's tenement John Thomasson (in pencil: by Shallcross mill); Gaskell's tenement Richard Gaskell (in pencil: Eccles Road); Kinder's tenement Joseph Kinder (in pencil: ditto sign); Wood's tenement George Wood; Over Close John Morten; Wheel House Isaac Fidler; Botany Milll Shallcross Manufactory; Horridge End four cottages nearly new (in pencil: Old Road); part of Reddish John Ibbitson, John Andrew and William Andrew Reddish = three houses; Taxal Lodge, George William Newton, Esq.; Lane Head [no occupant listed, but is also GWN]; Royal Oak Inn, James Collier near the Royal Oak, cottage etc John Lomas; Overton Demesne, G.W. Newton Esq; Great White Lee copse; Oak End Ebenezer Hill; Mill Stile Edward Heaps; Overton Mill Edward Heaps Mill-dam cottage; Madscar Martha Turner; Crowhill Henry Pearson, Moorside [no occupant listed[; Sitch Houses Joel Beard house, barn, stable, and cowhouse; part of Taxal Edge and Ladbitch, timber planted more than 35 years ago, principally larch fir; Black Hill Gate, Ebenezer Hill; Norman Wood, Ralph Pott; Knipe James Collier; Oldfield William Wilde farmhouse is ancient and substantial building; Master s James Wilson; Stubbins George Wilson; Intake Stephen Wilson; Intake Wood fir and young oaks 9 acres; Hoo Moor and part of Ladbitch has been planted 35 years and a great part of it is healthy and flourishing and thinnings easily sold at a fair price Moor and black game are plentiful; Within Leach William Hibbert; Goyt's Clough Daniel Downes; Hoo Moor plantation; Errwood James Poulson house, stable, barn, etc; .Goit's BridgeJohn Poulson house with pleasure grounds; Within Leach William Hibbert; Goyt's Clough Daniel Downes; Castedge Jeremiah Garlick 327 acres including 265 acres Shining Tor; Goyt's Moss stone quarry mill water wheel of cast iron, 60 ft in diameter for scouring flag in the two mills adjoining; Goit's Moss four cottages, other buildings in the same lot are principally new, 2 farm houses, 6 cottages, barn, etc and cabin for keeper when tenting on the moors well-stocked with game; Cat and Fiddle Inn Mrs Wain other buildings.

Chapter 5

A grim discovery

One of my grandmother's tales was of the body of a newborn child discovered at Taxal down by the Goyt, from where it had been brought back to the Royal Oak. My grandmother died in 1971. Almost fifty years later I decided to see if I could shed any more light on the story.

The newspapers soon got onto the story, and I was tempted to think that I could soon get to the bottom of this tragic incident by reading their reports. Far from it. But that should come as no surprise. One knows from one's experience of present-day newspaper practices that reports differ widely, even on fundamentals. Newspapers pick up a story at various stages in its development, with barely any of them offering a systematic, coherent account from start to finish. In this particular case the readers of a particular newspaper were often given tantalising brief glimpses, and that was that.

Nor can newspaper reports be relied upon to pay strict attention to the actual agenda followed at inquests and hearings. Consequently it is hard to know exactly who said what. Equally, even if one knows who wrote the report, it is difficult to assess the extent to which reporters and editors have imposed their own formulations, slant and conclusions on the proceedings described.

Despite all these handicaps or perhaps because of them it is a fascinating challenge to try to piece together this grim story, which will, I hope, strike present-day readers as just as tragic and traumatic for the woman involved as similar cases presented in the media today.

The story first surfaces on 28 April 1848 in the *Stockport Advertiser.* the report's heading: "Horrible Depravity Alleged case of child murder" primes the reader to expect a truly monstrous, unnatural crime.

On Friday last [i.e. Good Friday, 21 April] a young man called Collier had been going through a wood adjoining the Buxton turnpike road at Taxal near Whaley Bridge when he discovered the body of a newly born female child in "a small running water" near the river. "The child was quite dead." In contrast, in a second report in the *Derby Mercury* on 3 May, Collier is described as having been "groping for fish", i.e. tickling trout, in a small rivulet running through a clough, i.e a narrow valley with steep sides, known as Widow's Clough.

Widow's Clough

The first report goes on to describe the inquest conducted the next day at the Royal Oak before Charles Hudson, Esq. and "a respectable jury". Byron Booth, a surgeon from Chapel-en-le-Frith provides the principal evidence, which is presented here in a pretty random order, beginning, not ending, with his verdict. On the basis of his post mortem, his opinion was that the child had been born alive and could not have been more than two days old. Its weight was 9 lbs 10 oz, its length 21 inches. A narrow remnant of cloth was wrapped five or six times round its neck, at the end of which a slip noose was drawn so tight that the bandage had cut into its neck. The child had "evidently" been strangled in this way. (It is not at all clear whether these are his or the reporter's words.) The body was enveloped in a stuff apron, and a piece of cloth, tied tight behind its head, covered the child's mouth as if to prevent its cries being heard.

The jury, the report continues, were of the opinion that the child had been born in the neighbourhood and that, in view of its size, a third party was implicated. The coroner commented on "the barbarous manner in which the child had been put to death" and directed that the strictest enquiry be made. His verdict was un-ambiguous: it was a case of unlawful murder. Mr Andrews, the special chief constable for the division, the reader is informed, "has actively engaged, with every possibility of success, making the necessary enquiries as to the destination of the natural mother."

The second account, already referred to, that in the *Derby Mercury* and headed; "Shocking Case of Infanticide", makes its view of the incident clear from the start: it is one of those horrible cases of child murder which seem to be on the increase. It then turns to Matthew Collier's supposed evidence. Here the child is described as having been wrapped up like a bundle and stuck in a hole in the bank, close to the water, "as if concealed from view" - which suggests a deliberate act of concealment. Collier removed the bundle from its hiding place. On examination it turned out to be the body of a newborn female child, wrapped in a fine stuff apron and part of a petticoat. Round its neck was a shred of something which had "evidently" - again the word used in the first report - been put there for the purpose of strangulation, as it was very tight, "the face being flushed with blood and its little tongue protruding quite out of its mouth". Such distressing details were calculated to increase the revulsion felt by any decent-minded reader for the perpetrator's wicked and unnatural act. There is no mention here of a second piece of cloth.

It is hard to believe that the formulations and conclusions attributed to Collier, stem from him. He was, after all, a simple agricultural labourer. They sound much more either like Booth's or the reporter's. Collier, the report goes on, had instantly raised the alarm, and several people were soon at the spot. The body was conveyed to the house of Mr Henry Morten, i.e. to the Royal Oak, where Matthew was employed by his brother-in-law. In this second article all that is said of Byron Booth is that at the inquest, having conducted his post-mortem, he was of the decided opinion that the child, whose weight and size are again given, was full-term and had been born alive. It had, in his view, come to its end by foul means. Nothing is reported about the presumed date of death.

New is a reference to footprints made by a small, woman's shoe and traced along a lane nearby until the woman crossed a field leading to the clough. Has Andrews, the constable investigating the case, provided this information? A lane does lead from Taxal Church across to White Leas and it is just a short distance across a field to get down into the clough.

The woman appeared to have "jumped and fallen down a 'skeer' or rough place" in it. No proof is given for this assumption. Had her feet or her body left an imprint? Were "skid marks" visible? Was the turf or surface of the bank damaged?

The implicit assumption seems to be that the woman went down into the clough, carrying a newborn baby and intent on strangling it there. Supposedly the fall had not prevented her carrying out her heinous plan.Other explanations are possible, and I come to them later.

Footprints - presumably the same ones - "were also traced from the place by a different way". They, it was claimed, could only have been made after "the Wednesday previous, [i.e. the 12th], since, on that day, some parties had been "snigging" [i.e. roughly cutting down] timber at the spot. The existence of the footprints, the report goes on, leads to the "assumption" that the child had not been long murdered. From "assumption" it moves on to "facts": "The above-mentioned facts were all deposed before the coroner and jury, after which the inquest was then adjourned so that more information could be collected." "In the meantime", the report concludes, "the most rigorous investigation was to be made in order to bring to light the perpetrator of this horrible tragedy." In this interpretation the baby is the sole tragic figure; there is not the slightest suggestion that the "perpetrator" may be an equally tragic figure.

Nothing is said in this report of the necessary involvement of a third party, and, given that no male footsteps were found, it is hard to explain how, solely on the basis of the baby's size and weight, the jury could believe a third party had necessarily been involved.

The same day, 3 May, the *Stockport Advertiser* reported the verdict arrived at at the adjourned Inquest: "wilful murder by some person or persons unknown, no evidence having been tendered to incriminate any particular person." Clearly Andrews's investigations had led to nothing. The coroner, for his part, was only repeating his initial verdict.

By now the *Derbyshire Courier* was also onto the story. On Saturday, 6 May, it claimed that the previous week it had recorded the discovery near Taxal church of a new-born child in a hole by the water side. Yet, despite a long search I could not find any trace of any such report in its pages. Under the unequivocal heading "The case of child murder at Taxal" it informed its readers that Chief Constable Field - a police officer based in Ashbourne - had received information which had enabled him, together with a member of the county police, "to apprehend a woman in the Rookery, on suspicion of having murdered the child." It is not said where this "Rookery" is nor when the unnamed woman was apprehended, but she must have been released since we will subsequently learn that the woman accused of the crime at a later hearing was not arrested by Constable Field and a colleague but by Inspector Blood, and not until 24 May.

On 26 May another newspaper, the *Derbyshire Advertiser,* got onto the story. In its account of the petty sessions held on the 24th at Uttoxeter, it reported that Henry Millward (25), dressed in a sailor's garb and known in this and the adjoining counties as Leek Harry, had been brought up, together with Sarah Butcher (24). Both were tramps and had been apprehended by Inspector Blood as a result of an advertisement in the *Police Gazette*[1]. Butcher was charged with murdering her child on 21st ult. As the communication made to the magistrates was for the moment to remain private, the room was cleared, and the prisoners were remanded until Friday so that the necessary enquiries could be made.

This is the first time that a suspect has been named. Sarah Butcher, christened on 6 February 1825, was the daughter of William and Ann Butcher. Her father was a labourer; the family lived in Nethermoor, a part of Killamarsh, a township near Sheffield. Henry Millward was the son of John Millward, a labourer, and his wife Ann Millward. He and his siblings George William and Ann were living with their parents in Leek in 1841.

It was highly unlikely that the two would get a sympathetic hearing. The authorities and most "respectable" folk were anything but well disposed to "habitual tramps and vagrants who simulate destitution". Tramps were to be distinguished from the deserving poor and those who were temporarily and unavoidably in distress."[2] They were put into the same category as professional beggars, thieves, poachers, prostitutes and other scoundrels and should be dealt with by the police not by Poor

Law Boards. Their morals were allegedly infamous; they spread dangerous diseases; and their persons were disgustingly filthy. Workhouses should not readily distribute relief to persons not entitled to it.

On Saturday, 27 May, the *Staffordshire Advertiser* reported on the case under the heading "Charge of Infanticide". The report added nothing new.

It returned to the case on 17 June, reporting that Sarah Butcher had undergone her final examination at the Ram's Head, Disley before the Rev Peter Legh, J Grimshaw and J Newton. (This was the magistrates court that dealt with matters relating to Taxal.) All the reader is told is that she was committed for trial at the next assizes at Chester and "immediately forwarded on her way to that gaol." Millward, it seems, was discharged.

On Friday, 23 June, the *Chester Chronicle* provided some details about the hearing in Disley. Booth's evidence is not as hard as it was at the original inquest. Now it is only "as if" the mark found on the neck had been caused by something bound tightly round it. However, Booth does still go on to say that, in his opinion, the child had been born alive and had died from being suffocated by the ligature round the neck and the application of the cloth to the mouth. There were, the report goes on, other marks of violence on the body. A fracture on the skull must - presumably this is Booth's opinion - have been "inflicted before death by a blow", or was "the result of a crush". There was, however, no external injury to the skull.

In the meantime there had been developments in the police investigations. Three female witnesses, the report goes on, had seen Butcher "shortly before the 21st". She was, "large in the family way" and wearing a black apron similar to the one in which the baby was found. It is not said where they had seen her. At her later trial in Chester the vague location "in the neighbourhood of Taxal", will be provided. The police's investigations must have also taken them to a lodging house in Buxton, since another witness, Ann Robinson, its keeper, states that Butcher, who was known to her, had come to her house on Easter Monday, i.e. April 24. Robinson must have known of her pregnancy since she asked her what had happened to the baby. Butcher's reply was that she had "got her bed" on Shrove Tuesday, i.e. 7 March, at Winster, near Bakewell. When asked where the child was, her answer was that "our Harry beat and punched me so bad that the child was as black as a coal when it was born; so we were obliged to bury it." Even if this alleged birth at Winster is part of a changing account of events one does wonder whether Sarah was indeed subject to violence and abuse from Millward. Changing her tale, she had later told Robinson that she had been confined at Utcheter (Uttoxeter). This will be her claim from now on. Mr John Taylor Parsons, a surgeon from Stockport, said that he had examined her on 30 May. She looked as if she had been confined a few weeks previously. This hardly fitted her claim to have had the baby on Shrove Tuesday.

The Inspector of the Stafford County Constabulary - i.e. Inspector Blood then gave his evidence. He had apprehended Butcher on 24 May in a lodging house in Uttoxeter in the company of a man dressed as a sailor and commonly known as Leek Harry. Having searched her, he had taken her into custody on a charge of wilful murder. She told him that she had miscarried at the house on Ash Wednesday, i.e. 8 March. The lodging-house keeper corroborated this, claiming that she herself had buried the body in the garden in a piece of the accused's dress. On Friday the 26th Butcher had pointed out to Inspector Blood a place in the garden where the body had been buried. However, despite careful examination, nothing was found. "Some inconclusive evidence having been offered on behalf of the prisoner, she was committed to Chester Assizes to take her trial for child murder." There is nothing to indicate that Butcher had any legal representation at this hearing, and no information is provided as to who provided this inconclusive evidence or what it consisted of.

One needs to remember that a "common lodging house", also known as a doss house, was generally a grim place. Rarely was the accommodation provided something one could, by modern-day standards, equate with a decent, comfortable boarding-house. The rooms used as dormitories were often grossly overcrowded, squalid and ridden with vermin. In workhouses the regime was stricter and one had to perform work, but they were, I suspect, often cleaner. But a tramp like Sarah had perhaps good reasons to avoid knocking at the door of the workhouse in Chapel-en-le-Frith.

On 1 September the *Derbyshire Advertiser* returned to the case, reporting in some detail on the trial at Chester Assizes. On 24 August Sarah Butcher had been indicted for the wilful murder of her baby child by strangulation on 17 May. The date of the alleged murder has now been moved from the 21st to the 17th The account of the prosecution's case echoes the first account of the discovery: the body, the court is told, was found in a shallow brook. What is new is the information that by the time Booth conducted his post-mortem, the constables had already removed the bandages. The information that the child had been tied up in a black apron with some pieces of a puce coloured dress tied over its mouth and a bandage of brown Holland tied very tightly round its neck can only stem from them. There was, according to Booth, a deep red mark where the strip had been and some clotted blood in the child's mouth and throat; the lungs had been dilated; the general appearance of the body seemed to be healthy.

His view was that the blood in the baby's mouth and throat could have been there even had it been born dead, but not with the lungs so dilated as they were. Nor, in his view, was the slight fracture on the baby's head sufficient to cause death. This he attributed, as he had consistently done right from the start, to strangulation caused by the ligature round the neck. The way in which he presents his evidence strongly suggests that he was well aware that if the charge of infanticide were to be upheld, it had to be proved that the child had been born alive and was, to use the terminology of the time, "entirely separated alive from the mother".[3] If this could not be proved, the lesser charge of concealment often replaced it. The body was, he said, quite fresh when he examined it and he was of the opinion that it must have been born within four days. His initial assessment had been "not more than two days before". At this point the judge himself raises with him the crucial question of whether the child was definitely alive at birth. Booth, who till now had been so decided in his opinion that it had, admits that it might have breathed when partially delivered but been dead when full born. He also concedes that the injury to the child's head might have been caused while the prisoner was delivering herself.

The report now brings evidence somewhat different from that provided at the hearing at the Ram's Head. Butcher had been identified by two females, who claim to have "relieved" her, when, on 17 April, she was begging in the neighbourhood of Taxal, in an advanced state of pregnancy. At the hearing in Disley three women, all unnamed, had stated that they had seen her "shortly before the 21st". The two in court are now much more precise. Was, one wonders, this certainty on their part one of the reasons why the date of the supposed murder has been brought back to the 17th? Butcher, they claim, had told them that she expected to be delivered soon, as she was in the last month of her pregnancy. Ann Robinson, although not here named, must be the person who then "shows" that Butcher had been at a lodging house in Buxton on 24 April, in very delicate health. She repeats the evidence she gave at the Ram's Head: knowing Butcher had been pregnant, she had asked her where the baby was, Butcher's answer had been that she had miscarried.

From now on one has a strong feeling that the reporter or editor is running out of time or space or both, because the further proceedings are dealt with very cursorily indeed. Butcher, the reader is told, had not been apprehended till about 20 May in Uttoxeter. Hitherto the date has always been precise: the 24th.

Once again her landlady in Uttoxeter "swore positively" that Butcher had miscarried on 8 March and that the foetus, about two months old, had been buried in the garden.

All that the reader is then told is that that the judge summed up very clearly. Frustratingly, no details of his summary are provided. He had left the jury to decide if the prisoner had given birth to the child and if so, whether it had met its death from the violence of the prisoner.

The report's ending could hardly be more stark: "Verdict: Not Guilty".

Perhaps this outcome is the explanation why the final stages of the case are dealt with so briefly. Was the reporter expecting a guilty verdict? Was his hope or confidence that the judge's summing up would be damning for Sarah. Would readers be confirmed in their conviction that this was indeed another of the growing number of infanticides, in fact one of the most horrifying and unnatural? Was the not guilty verdict, therefore, a disappointment, a terrible anti-climax? Was it now just a case of a tramp getting off lightly? Many readers would have shared that feeling.

What might have swayed the jury's verdict? Had the judge's two reminders, first to Booth and then to the jury, had an effect? Even if jurors may have been sceptical of Butcher's and the Uttoxeter lodging house keeper's accounts of the date and place of the alleged miscarriage and burial of the baby, and even if they may have held her to be the person who had deposited a body in the brook or bank at Taxal, were they nevertheless not convinced beyond reasonable doubt that, whatever else she had intended or done, she had not wilfully murdered a living baby? Did they consider it possible that the baby had not necessarily died because of her violence.

If they deemed it possible that she had gone down into the clough and fallen, were they perhaps ready to believe that she may not have been carrying a baby at all. Could not the fall have brought on childbirth, forcing her to deliver herself? Might not the baby have been injured by the fall or during the delivery and died then or soon afterwards? Was an even more gruesome scenario not possible? In her physical distress, emotional confusion, and desperation about her situation as a homeless, penniless beggar, abused by her violent partner, might she not have felt that she had no alternative but to strangle her child? Even more horrendous – might she have attempted to strangle a baby already dead?

It would be heartening to think that even for an all-male jury of respectable citizens a guilty verdict would have been just one step too far.
I wonder what my grandmother's verdict would have been. That we will never know.

Notes

1. Not all the years of the *Police Gazette* have been preserved, and Find my Past has digitised it only down to 1829.

2. *Chester Chronicle* 25.8. 48

3. See Baron Alderson's address to the Grand Jury at South Lancashire Assizes , reported in the *Liverpool Standard* on 28 March 1848

Chapter Six

The Royal Oak and goings-on in Taxal

The days when there was a public house at Taxal are long gone. I remember top-of-the-range cars being driven to it along the Linglongs in the 1950s. By that time the Royal Oak, modernised after the Second World War, had been renamed the Chimes of Taxal by the owner, Mr DeSachs, who turned it into an expensive country restaurant where wealthy business men like Sir Vincent de Ferranti wined and dined their wives and lady friends. The five bedrooms were, I am told, well-used. Suits were prescribed for the saloon bar, while hikers and others were banished to a bar on the side. If locals just wanted a drink, there were cheaper, less pretentious pubs in Horwich End to go to. But it did have its local devotees: Freddy Yarker, head down, darting along, often with a book under his arm and a torch in his hand, Hughie Boothy, a man of jumbled words and shaking head, stumbling along, all over the place, Jack Pheasey, squeaky-voiced, serenely wobbling along, his large white-shirted belly proudly framed by his braces. To us boys they all seemed happier on the way back than on the way there.

Early publicans

The Royal Oak had originally been a farm. Farm buildings and at least one little cottage survived late into the second half of the nineteenth century.

Extract from the 1849 map of the Royal Oak. The two cottages are occupied by George Taylor and John Collier

These buildings were knocked down to make way for a large coach house. A large room above it catered for meetings and large dinners. The building was converted into private residences in the 1980s.

The bath has long since disappeared

Since it is referred to as Pownalls Farm in the Land Tax records for the years 1826 to 1831, the Royal Oak was presumably once occupied by the Pownalls, an old Taxal family mentioned in the early church records. Edward Taylor is the first publican at the farm whom I have been able to trace. Born in Lancashire about 1750, he married in 1771 a girl from Chapel-en-le-Frith, Mary Lomas, and together they had twelve children.

In 1790 Taylor figures in the letter already quoted from John Dickenson jun. about the half-yearly audit meeting at which tenants paid their rents at the inn.

Taylor, who was sexton at St James's for 23 years, died in 1806. His widow then ran the inn for several years. On 15 February 1809, one of his daughters, Louisa, married James Collier, a young widowed farmer and carpenter, whose father farmed at

Knipe.

He took over from his mother-in-law. Elizabeth, my great-great-grandmother, was baptised at Taxal on August 4 1811. She married Henry Morten, the third son of John Morten (1773-1829), a member of the Morten family from Chapel- en-le-Frith. Originally a farmer on the Silk Hill, John became the tenant of Shallcross Hall Farm and looked after the Hall itself, when the absentee Jodrells were struggling to find a buyer or tenant for it in the 1820s. Henry, who was born on July 8 1812 and baptised on August 13 at Chapel-en-le-Frith, initially worked at Shallcross for his father as an agricultural labourer. Elizabeth Collier thus lived a stone's throw away on the other side of the Goyt valley. In 1832 she gave birth to his son, Joseph Morten Collier. The couple married two years later in Cheadle, not, as one would have normally expected, at Taxal. Nancy was born at the end of 1836 when Henry was still a labourer at Shallcross, but the couple seem to have moved soon afterwards to the Royal Oak, where Henry helped his father-in-law with the farm till James died in 1840. The couple had eight more children: Ralph, Mary, John, Elizabeth, Sarah, Henry, Martha, and Edward. Ralph, in time, became the tenant of Reddish Farm, where the Mortens farmed for many years.

Reddish Farm

Edward became a teacher at the Taxal Church Day School, marrying another teacher there, the daughter of the village shoemaker, Robert Heathcote. He later went into the cutlery business in Sheffield. The girls mainly married farmers. In the district

Users and customers

The Jodrells used the inn for estate affairs. Now that Foster Bower's plantations were maturing, their land agent, Joseph Hudson Beswick had two notices announcing the sale of timber. inserted in the *Manchester Courier* in December 1834, Mr Collier would "shew" the various lots and provide printed particulars.

In 1840 Beswick had cause for grave concern. Strikingly highlighted by unusually large, heavy print, a £20 reward - something over £2,000 in today's terms - was offered in the *Macclesfield Courier* on 7 March for information leading to the conviction of some evil disposed person or persons who had on Wednesday night or early on Thursday morning last, wilfully and maliciously set on fire at Taxal the plantations belonging to John William Jodrell. The *Liverpool Mail* on 10 March reported that they had been set alight at four places. Although the fire raged over about 100 acres, the prevailing wind luckily meant comparatively little damage was caused. Otherwise almost 1000 acres could have been affected. Tempting as it must have been, the reward did not induce any informant to come forward.

On his visits to Taxal, Beswick used as his office a little cottage close to the plantations, "Moorside".

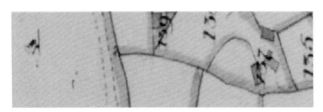

Tithe map of 1844 showing Moor Road and "Moorside"(139) on the left of the track leading from Moor Road to Crowhill Farm (137)

On December 6 1840 Moses and Mary Ann Jackson brought my great grandfather William from Kettleshulme to Taxal to be christened at St James's. Even if money was extremely tight, the party would have called in at the Royal Oak afterwards. Was it talk heard here that alerted Moses to the pickings to be had were he to break into "Moorside"? Being so remote, it was an easy, safe target since Beswick only occupied it when supervising the felling of timber.

The break-in had dire consequences for Moses. These I describe in the Kettleshulme book.

In the same month, on December 20 1840, the Mortens had their third son, John, christened. One of his daughters, Jessie, would marry one of William's sons, my grandfather, John Arthur Jackson.

Whereas public houses in Whaley Bridge and Horwich End faced stiff competition from a large number of inns and beer houses, themselves often struggling to survive, the Royal Oak had no worries on that score. Besides the income derived from the farm, it enjoyed the great advantage of being close to the church. As a result it was much used by those attending baptisms, confirmations, weddings and funerals. For its day-to-day trade it relied on faithful, thirsty farmers and farm labourers from the farms roundabout. My grandmother's tales, though from a later period in Queen Victoria's reign, would be true of the earlier period too. With money in their pockets from a sale, farmers often went "on the spree", staying at the inn "till the money was done". Then, if need be, the lethargic dozers were helped into their carts and traps, the horse given a tap on its rump, and off it trotted back to the farm with its master. After a funeral farmers would also stay at the inn for days on end. As a girl, my grandmother greeted a council worker, Elijah Ford, but got no reply. Her mother's explanation for his silence was simple: he had been at the inn for a fortnight and spent a lot of money there. Another of her tales was of a farmer climbing over a style, singing "trim your lamps and be ready for behold the bridegroom comes." Whether the "bride" would be so delighted by his arrival is another matter. In Taxal the temperance cause did number among its supporters a few non-conformist farmers like the Wesleyan, Benjamin Frost, who farmed at Sitch House, but they were few and far between.

Sitch House early in the last century

My grandmother was told by her father that there had earlier been a "bear croft" where the car park now is. The "sport" of having vicious dogs bait a bear chained to a post was banned in 1835, but many of our ancestors would themselves have had no time for the RSPCA or the League against Cruel Sports. In 1834 the licence of Taylor, the publican at the White Hart in Whaley Bridge, was not renewed because of a horrific case of bull baiting.[1] While researching for his book *Derbyshire Days,* which appeared in 1926 a signed copy of which he gave to the Mortens, H. M. Leach, spent time at Sitch House, and it was perhaps there that he was alerted, not just to bull and bear-baiting at the Royal Oak, but also to prize-fighting. On page 31 he writes:

> *On the smooth meadow below the inn sometimes as many as three fights would be in progress – six on 'em agät an onst – and the tale is told of a day when the fun grew so fast*

and furious that the constable, a farmer living at the very house of which I write, was sent for to restore order. In due course the constable arrived, drank a mug or two of ale to warm himself for action, and was soon fighting indiscriminately like the rest.

On April 15 1837 the *Manchester Times* reported that James Collier, described as a retail beer seller, had been reported at Stockport Petty Sessions for allowing gaming in his house on March 22. A constable stated that ten men were drinking in the house, while four were playing cards. The magistrates strongly "reprobated" the defendant's conduct but, since a note from the clergyman at Taxal gave him a good character, he got off lightly, paying a penalty of 20/-, including costs. If James was indeed only a "beer seller", that would have meant that he could not sell spirits.

Inquests were held at the inn. For example, the inquest in 1848 into the death of the newborn baby girl whose corpse was found in Widow's Clough was conducted there, as was, in 1868, that of a six-year old boy who, having fallen asleep in a cart taking coal back to Bonsall from a colliery in Whaley Bridge, had tumbled onto the road at Taxal Wood and had his head crushed under a wheel.[2] Ten years later an inquest was conducted on William Brocklehurst of Knipe Farm.[3] On the day of his funeral the new hearse belonging to Jonathan Proctor, rolled down the hill on its way to collect his body and was "smashed very much". Somehow it still managed to transport the body to the church. After the burial service many a pint of ale would have been leisurely supped as the significance of this misadventure was sagely mulled over.

William was succeeded at Knipe by his son George, who died in 1906. He, in his turn, was followed by his son James who, in 1911, is recorded as working as a sawyer on the Jodrell Estate. Living with him are his elder brother George, a "woodman", and his sister Dinah. She acts as housekeeper for the two. Dinah, who never married, was one of my grandmother's childhood friends. Oakenend was, after all, only a stone's throw away from Knipe. Late in the Great War she took her children to see Dinah who, in the meantime, had moved across to Normanwood. They were under strict orders to eat up whatever they were given. Dinah gave my father a slice of thickly buttered, fresh bread. Used, as he was, to war-time rations, despite being ravenously hungry, he could not cope with such rich food. Fearing to get into bother, he bided his time and then stuffed the slice of bread up his jumper. Dinah's comment on noticing his empty plate: "Jessie, that boy's eaten his bread and butter already." The sticky truth came out on the way home. The memory stuck with him.

My grandmother also knew well the Wilsons, members of which family are recorded as having lived at Dowry Farm, Stubbins, Masters, Intack and Oldfield. Sarah Wilson, a widow, lived at neighbouring Madscar with her two girls, Mary Alice and Eliza, Maurice Lomas's grandmother.

The Wilsons at Madscar Farm

Eliza's brother Robert, was at Madscar in 1911, moved out and later, having worked on the railways, came back to live just across the clough at Knipe, the farm where James Collier sen. had farmed over a century before.

The two sisters in their typically late Victorian "best". Their waistlines could hardly be trimmer

Knipe Farm

Robert Wilson

A premature interment

James Collier died late in 1840, aged 65. Aided by his forceful mother-in-law, Henry Morten officially took control of the inn. During the 1840s an incident involving it swept through the newspapers and was reported even in Ireland.[4]

One Saturday evening, not long ago, a man who had been making a little too free with John Barleycorn had to pass through the Taxal churchyard where a deep grave had been dug for an interment on the morrow, close to the

footpath over which the jocose fellow had to pass on his way home, and being rather unsteady in his gait and not quite able to maintain his true perpendicular, he unfortunately fell into the grave, and being unable to get out again, he quietly resigned himself to his fate and went to sleep. Shortly afterwards, one of his boon companions, in passing the same way, had the misfortune to fall into the same grave and rouse the first occupant from his sleep, who, feeling offended at the intruder's visit, uttered out in an angry growl, "It's strange one cannot lie quietly in the grave." These words, being uttered in a somewhat ghostly tone, so frightened the intruder that he quickly scaled the walls of the clay tenement and scampered away as fast as his legs could carry him to his friends he had just left at the public house, to whom he told the story of his misadventure, the recital of which roused the people's curiosity, and they resolved to go, in a body, to the grave , and if possible ascertain from whence sprung the apparent supernatural voice which had so terrified their informant. Accordingly, with fear and trembling, they proceeded to the grave and found it occupied by a faithful pot-companion who had lately left their company, whom they quickly liberated from his cold dormitory, to the infinite amusement of all present.[5]

A parson and six petticoats

In 1854 Taxal got a new rector. In search of a living, the Rev John Goode Slight turned to an agency that specialised in dealing in benefices. St James's was on the market at £3,500. Slight concluded a deal. Having bought the advowson, i.e. become patron of the church and thereby entitled to recommend or appoint a clergyman of his choice, he "presented" himself to the Bishop of Chester. He then refused to pay the 10% fee which he owed the agent, and was taken to court - unsuccessfully. This was the beginning of a string of articles in major newspapers, which over the years cited Taxal as a notorious example of simony, i.e. the buying and selling of ecclesiastical preferments and benefices[6].

Slight's introduction to the parish was not a felicitous one in other respects either. On January 6 1855, under the heading "Incivility in the Church", the *Manchester Times* published a letter from "A Working Man" complaining that he had attended divine service at Taxal and that during the whole time nobody had provided him with a hymn book or allowed him to share theirs.

In the 1860s, aged 16, my great-grandmother, Martha Green, came from Pilsbury near Hartington to be lady's maid to Mrs Slight. She remembered having been told off for having forgotten one of Mrs Slight's six petticoats while helping to dress her: "My child you have forgotten something." Despite this oversight the Slights took to her: "If you'll call me mother, all my jewels will be yours." They even wanted to adopt her. She was less keen on the idea, later telling my grandmother that she only married John Morten to escape from them. Piqued, Slight told her that he would not marry her but he would bury her. He did neither.

A garden party at the rectory a century later. Round the table: Catherine Day, Andrew Morten. David Hartley, Stephen Fletcher (now in Aberdeen), David Slater (now in Australia), Phillip Day. Anything but a Victorian gathering.

A much less draughty and more environment-friendly ex-rectory
in October 1921

In 1875, in poor health, Slight tried to sell the advowson but failed
to get the price he wanted. So he stayed on in the rectory, leaving
his curate to carry out his duties. After his death in 1878 his
widow appointed the Rev W Whitworth, a man already in his
seventies and clearly intended to serve as a "warming pan" or
"caretaker" until the son or nephew of the prospective buyer, a
Buxton hotel keeper, Brian Bates, was ready to take over. Whitworth was installed and Bates bought the advowson. But Bates
died soon afterwards and, as a result, his plans went awry. Whitworth, who proved a much more committed and popular rector
than Slight had ever been, lived on as rector to a ripe old age. His
grave, like that of his son, is at the top of the lower graveyard not
far from that of his successor, the legendary Rev Samuel Evans.

Tourists and visitors

In 1828 the *Morning Post* published in instalments the account of
a walk from Manchester to London. On 18 September the wayfarer
walks from Manchester to Buxton. From Whaley he goes down
the valley and over a "brook" to Taxal, "this sweetly sequestered

place".

The Curate lives in a white house, with its bright casements
peeping under the branches of dark firs and tall poplars.
The sexton also lives close by, and keeps a small public
house. He was not at home, but his good woman was, and I
found her busy in household affairs; three or four fine
children were playing on the clean hearth, and a large mug
of cream stood in the chimney- nook, previous to its being
churned. Took a draught of her "own brewing"; it was
very good, and drank like that which I got at home

In the churchyard he notes down various epitaphs. The first to
catch his eye reads:

Friend, do not, careless, on thy road,
O'erlook this humble shrine;
For, if thou art a friend of God,
Here lies a friend of thine.

The second is on the grave of an infant who died aged four:

O, parents dear, mourn not
For her that you have lost,
Nor yet be over sad;
The fewer days she lived on earth
The fewer faults she had.
The fewer years she lived below,
The longer is her rest,
GOD call'd her hence in early day,
Because he thought it best.

From 1857 onwards, with the completion of the railway line from
Manchester, visitors increasingly came to Whaley Bridge in order
to embark there on excursions by carriage, coach and trap to
Buxton, Castleton and other places in the Peak District. Although
the hamlet of Taxal did not lie on their direct route, they could
get a glimpse of it as they climbed up Long Hill. It is no surprise
therefore that it figures in feuilleton articles as more and more

escaped from the smoke and grime there. On 5 July 1856, the *Ashton Weekly Reporter* carried a piece by Salmagundi entitled "A ramble to Buxton". It painted an idyllic picture of Whaley Bridge and Taxal.

> *Rambles in the country, far away from the smoke of towns, not only exhilarate the spirits and recreate you, but undoubtedly create a higher sense for all that is beautiful in Nature and in Art but also fit us more earnestly to 'Follow Nature up to Nature's God'.*

The party sets off in Stockport, and, having passed scores of navvies making an "iron road" at Disley, hears explosions as they blast the solid rock.

> *This railway is to connect Stockport and Whaley Bridge and will doubtless be carried on to Buxton and through the heart of Derbyshire itself. Should this be done it will, of course, prove of incalculable advantage to that county, as the only means of transport is at presentthe carriage and the lurry.*

At Whaley Bridge the party gets out and goes to the White Hart. The fare sorely disappoints them. None of them, the reader is told, will ever forget the deaf waiter, the almost butterless bread and the weak tea. Leaving

The White Hart

soon after six, they find the road, i.e. the present-day A5004 along Long Hill - very tiresome since the rain has turned the soft limestone into a thick slippery paste. But the scenery for a mile or two is described as exceedingly picturesque and beautiful.

The hills, to their right, forming Taxal Edge, rise gently for some hundreds of feet and are dotted with clusters of dark firs.

> *Then another delightful picture before us. There in the silent valley below is Whaley [Taxal!] Church, embosomed within trees, with a babbling brook [the Goyt!] flowing gently beside; behind are the greenhills looking cheerful even in their sullenness. Near the church are a few plain cottages where children are frisking about in all their innocence and simplicity.*

Clearly the party did not have time to make the little detour down to the Goyt and up Church Brow to the Royal Oak. They toil along Long Hill in the thick atmosphere and reach Buxton at 8.30, having been over 8 hours on their journey.

Elisabeth Morten had died at the Royal Oak on May 10 1855, aged 43. A flat tombstone below the east window of the church bears the inscription:

> *Dear husband now my life is past.*
> *You faithful loved me to the last*
> *Grieve not for me but pity take*
> *On my children for my sake.*

The Morten grave is one of the graves under the eastern window. The lower graveyard has not long been opened, and the extensive changes made to the church when the Rev Samuel Evans was rector still belong to the future.

In 1857 Henry married again, this time a farmer's widow, Jane Lomas. She was well-suited to carrying on the farm-cum-inn, and things went on as before. Thus on 9 June 1860 the *Glossop Record* reports on the half- yearly audit of Squire Jodrell's rents. The tenantry, it noted, did ample justice to the excellent dinner provided:

> *Much credit is due to the host and hostess of the Royal Oak, Taxal, for the attention they pay to these occasions, having a good dinner, with a plentiful supply of "John Barleycorn", for, as these audits are looked forward to for sometime, nothing is wanting on the part of the host and hostess to make the tenants feel jovial.*

At the Jodrell Arms Mrs Ward offered similar fare. There was no place on such occasions at either hostelry for vegetarian and temperance ideas.[7] Roast beef and plum pudding reigned supreme in the realm of John Bull. Fittingly, a song popular at the time was "The Old Roast Beef of England"

One suspects that alcohol consumed at the Royal Oak was involved in a "fearful accident" that occurred after a wedding at the church in 1865 and was reported in a host of newspapers. The drivers of the two cars, probably with a drink or two inside them, could not agree who should take the lead on the way back to Whaley Bridge. A race ensued. Unfortunately one of the cars did not succeed in negotiating the corner at the White Horse in Horwich End. After running on one wheel for a considerable distance, it "upset, throwing the occupants into the road with great violence". There they lay, in shock, injured, some unconscious, including the parish clerk, Isaac Lomas. Eventually they did all come round, but in the case of Miss Eliza Waine, the daughter of the bridegroom's father, the prominent Whaley Bridge farmer, Abel Waine, it was not until the next day that she "showed signs of animation" and uttered a few words. It was feared that her spine was permanently injured.[8]

Welcome extra income at the inn was provided by the visits made by large groups like the Oddfellows, Rifle Volunteers and other societies in the course of their processions and parades to St James's. Attendance at divine service became an integral part of these anniversary celebrations. In 1840, the Independent Order of Oddfellows assembled at the Soldier Dick in Furness Vale, walked in procession to Taxal and enjoyed an excellent dinner at the inn.[9] Similarly, in August 1864, 100 members and friends of the Furness Vale Mutual Improvement Society and Reading Room formed a procession and, honoured by the presence of some female friends, proceeded, with banners and band, to the Furness Lodge, the grand house of Mr Saxby, the owner of the printworks.

Furness Lodge. Demolished in the 1970s

Having taken refreshments there, they set off for the Royal Oak - a considerable distance. Their exertions were rewarded: "A sumptuous tea was provided, the whole company sitting down at once." Henry's mother-in-law, Louisa Collier, was not going to miss out on being the star of the occasion:

> *A venerable old lady who has resided in that house all her lifetime was invited to partake of tea and in the course of her conversation she informed the company that she was a grandmother to forty children and great-grandmother to nine; she is*

about 80 years of age, hale and hearty and every
appearance of attaining a still greater age. When tea
was concluded, the company, young and old, joined in a
variety of games on the "green", with an occasional
dance and song. Mr Charles White of Stalybridge sang
"The roast beef of old England" in a capital style. "The
weather being all that each could desire, they enjoyed
themselves till dusk.[10]

Infringements of the licensing laws

As the temperance movement gained supporters in the 1860s
and 1870s, more fines were imposed on errant publicans. Repeat-
ed offences could lead to the suspension of a victualler's
licence. Henry Morten fell foul of the law in 1865. At the
County Petty Sessions in Stockport he was summoned for having
company in his house after 10.00 o'clock on the morning of
Sunday, November 5. A policeman said that he foundfour men,
each drinking a glass of ale. Morten admitted the fact and also
that they had had some bread and cheese. As he had kept the
house for 33 years without a single complaint, he was only called
upon to pay the costs.[11] He must have breathed a sigh of relief.

In 1870, realising his time was up, Henry made his will on June 7.
At some stage Jane had died and he had married a mysterious
Hannah. I could find no trace of the marriage, but one of his
executors is his "brother-in-law, Elias Joule. Hannah could, therefore, be Hannah Joule, born in 1839 to William and Elizabeth
Joule of Taxal. References in the will to monies which are only to
be paid to his widow if she gives birth to a child within eight
months of his demise, if she does not re-marry, or if her conduct
is deemed satisfactory to his executors, do not suggest that Henry
was totally convinced that his third wife, who was much younger,
would long remain a widow or not "carry on" with somebody
else. Less than a month later, on July 4, he was dead. He was
buried on the 8th. Louisa Collier, his mother-in-law, soon followed him. She was buried on the 28th. She was 84.

Henry's son Henry took over the inn. The beginning of his reign was not auspicious. At the Stockport County Brewster [Licensing] Sessions at the end of August it was alleged that on March 6 he had been fined the sum of 10/- and costs for Sunday trading. In the chairman's view, this was a rather bad case: he must take warning and not offend similarly next year; otherwise he could count on it that his licence would be withdrawn.[12]

Henry's marriage on February 6, 1872 to Mary Hannah King, the daughter of a Whaley Bridge draper, got him into more hot water. Eight days later, on Wednesday, the 14th, at the Stockport County Petty Sessions, he is summoned for having committed an offence against the tenor of his licence on the 7th. At the hearing hilarity soon becomes the order of the day. Sergeant Naylor, for the prosecution, declares that, at about 2.15 a.m., he had visited the house with Sergeant Porter. Before going in, they had seen a man outside vomiting, "having come out of the passage in that state". Inside they found one man laid down on the settle, quite drunk; another man was holding himself by the partition in another room; through the bar were several other men, all of whom seemed very drunk; in another room on the left of the passage another man was asleep and apparently very drunk. Having called the attention of the landlord to the drunken state of the company, the police left. Morten ran after them for about 100 yards and begged them, this one time, to overlook the matter. There were, Sergeant Naylor continues, about ten persons drunk and some 16 to 18 in the house. In answer to Mr Johnson, acting for the defence, Sergeant Naylor states that Morten had been married and this was the wedding party, adding: "In one room through the bar there was dancing to the strains of a concertina, but there was no disorderly conduct whatever." The mood in the court is by now very relaxed: "Amidst much amusement" he describes the appearance of the men: "they seemed drowsy and their heads did not hang very steadily on their necks." This is greeted with laughter. The landlord, he adds, was sober, indeed he was the only one who seemed perfectly so. From now on the laughs continue:

Mr Johnson:	"You say they were vomiting through being drunk; now,
Sergeant:	I daresay you have vomited many a time without being drunk." (Laughter)
Clerk (jocosely):	"And with dancing too, Mr Johnson." (Laughter)

Sergeant Porter, having corroborated Naylor's evidence, is cross examined by Mr Johnson, who asks what statement the landlord made as to the house being open so long.

Witness:	"He said he had been married that day.
"Mr Johnson:	"Are you married, Sergeant?"
Witness:	"Yes."
Mr Johnson:	"And I daresay you had a jollification at your wedding, did you not?"
Witness:	" Not in a public house, sir." (Laughter)
Clerk:	"Publicans, you know, have no other house to go to." (Laughter).

After a few more humorous exchanges the magistrates dismiss the case on the grounds that most of the company were friends whom the landlord had invited to the wedding.[13]

A good time was clearly had by all except the two policemen who had been made to squirm.

Gamekeepers and poachers

Hunting had always been the preserve of the aristocracy, and self-made men like Samuel Grimshaw at neighbouring Errwood proudly spent large sums developing the hunting, shooting and fishing facilities on their estates. Landowners and those who had

Gamekeepers and workers on the Errwood
Estate in 1881

bought shooting rights from them ruthlessly enforced these rights, including against their own tenant farmers. As one might expect, incidents involving poaching are reported with a frequency and an attention to detail difficult for us to imagine today.

Henry Morten's brother, John, my great-grandfather, became one of Samuel Grimshaw's considerable team of gamekeepers at Errwood Hall and moved into Castedge Cottage with his young bride in 1871. He was a small, sturdy man, who, when he got older, insisted on always having a large shirt hung on the washing line so that poachers and thieves would think the occupant of the farm big and burly. He was not averse to dealing violently with any poachers he apprehended.

He knew well William Hulse. Hulse had worked for the Grimshaws for a time but then joined the Jodrell team. Reports in local papers of prosecutions he brought against poachers illustrate well that side of a gamekeeper's duties. At Buxton Petty Sessions in 1861 he summoned James Newton of Chapel-en-le-Frith for shooting a rabbit on the Manor of Taxal. Newton was fined 15/- and costs or 15 days imprisonment.[14]

In 1863 Hulse summoned an old offender, Nathaniel Ogden, from Bridgemont, whom he had caught with 30 live trout at a pond in Taxal. Ogden was fined 40/-and costs or two months' imprisonement. Being unable to pay, Ogden, who, the report goes on, had caught more fish than any man in North Derbyshire, was sent to Derby.[15]

Throughout the 1860s Hulse lived close to the Royal Oak in one of the Lodge Wood Cottages and thus next door to John's relatives, the Colliers. John followed his example in moving over to the Jodrells. In fact it may have been Hulse's retirement that created an opening for him.

Lodge Wood Cottages (Photo: Peter Slack)

John Morten figures in quite a number of newspaper reports.

In 1875 two shoemakers from Macclesfield, George (54) and John Coates (58) were charged at Stockport County Police Court with unlawfully being on land at Taxal hired for shooting from the Jodrells by Major Brookes of Leicester. It was claimed that on the night of September 12 1875 they had with them nets, bags, etc. for the purpose of taking game. They were also charged with assaulting John Morten. In giving evidence for the prosecution, he stated that he was on duty with three others at the bottom of the Taxal Edge covert [i.e. trees, undergrowth and bushes that shelter game] when they saw a number of men there. He went towards them, saw George Coates, and shouted to his companions: "Chaps, now come up." Coates made an attempt to strike him on the head with his stick, but he warded off the blow and received it on the shoulder. He then raised his own stick and felled Coates to the ground. While one of his companions seized Coates, he turned his attention to the others. When John Coates struck him, "he served him as the other prisoner", striking him to the ground. Some five other men ran away. Each of the prisoners had a bag; in George's were six live rabbits, in John's, two. They also had 17 set rods and a large stick apiece. A long net was found in George's coat pocket, and on the ground nearby lay a third bag with half a dozen live rabbits in it.

Mr Brown, representing the defendants, based his case on claiming that Morten had used excessive violence.

> Mr Brown: "And you belaboured them pretty well didn't you?"
>
> Witness: "In self-defence."
>
> Mr Brown: "You belaboured a man so much a short time ago that you had to pay £ 35 to settle it."
>
> Witness: "No, I did not."
>
> Mr Brown: "Did nobody for you?"
>
> Witness : "No."
>
> Mr Brown: "Do you mean to say that in January last you did not break a man's jaw?"
>
> Witness: "No."

Mr Brown: "Did you damage him?"

Witness: "Well, it was never proved.
Mr Brown: "Do you know a man named Sellars? Did
            you break his jaw?"
Witness: "I know him well. And he robbed me on
            the highway."
Mr Brown: "Did you break his jaw?"
Witness: "No."
Mr Brown: "Was his jaw broken?"
Witness: "No, it was not."
Mr Brown: "Did you pay a sum of money to
            settle the proceedings he
            instituted against you?"
Witness: "Well, I did pay a sum."
Mr Brown: "How much?"
Witness: "£12."
Mr Brown: "That was in self-defence?"
Witness: "Well, I paid that."
Mr Brown: "And you say you belaboured these men
            in self-defence? How many of you were
            there?"
Witness: "Four of us."

In reply to further questions Morten admitted that the three wounds on George Coates's head and the one on the other prisoner's head were caused by his violence. The two had, he claimed, been so "resolute" that he had had to strike them in order to capture them. John Goddard, a stonemason living at Horwich End and acting as a "nightwatchman" for Major Brookes, gave similar evidence: When they first went up to the prisoners, they and their companions were standing with sticks in their hands, ready to strike them. When George Coates was on the floor, he had seized hold of Morten's throat and Morten had given him a tap on the head with his stick. Some tap! Richard Bennett, another gamekeeper, confirmed this evidence.

Constable Burr said that he was sent for and went to the Royal Oak, where Morten delivered the men into his custody. He had found on them net hooks, a long net and a dog-slip for the dog which George Coates had with him. On the way to Disley, John Coates had said to him: "We can't deny we was on the ground but we hadn't got a single rabbit off then."

The prisoners were granted bail and committed for trial,[15]

They duly appeared at the Cheshire Spring Assizes in early March and were both sentenced to nine months' hard labour. My great grandfather, who liked his drink, would have returned to a hero's welcome at the Royal Oak.

This was a time of acute economic distress, not just in large towns like Macclesfield, but also in villages like Whaley Bridge, where a soup kitchen was organised in the winter of 1879. In contrast, those in possession of shooting rights continued to bag game in abundance. Thus in 1882 a large party of gentlemen including Major Brookes and MrGaskell jun. of Ingersley Hall, with twelve guns, shot enough rabbits, grouse and other game in Taxal Wood to fill large bags.

The water mill and "Monkey"

In the early 1870s John Morten moved to Mill Clough, a farm standing in the deep clough that runs down to the Goyt from Hoo Moor and passes below three farms, Overton, Oakenend and Madscar, on the one side, and two others, Normanwood and Knipe, on the other.

.In the seventeenth-century several inventories of the property owned by the Downes family mention a watermill. Was it, one wonders, the one that at this time stood in the clough just below their ancestral home, Overton Hall?

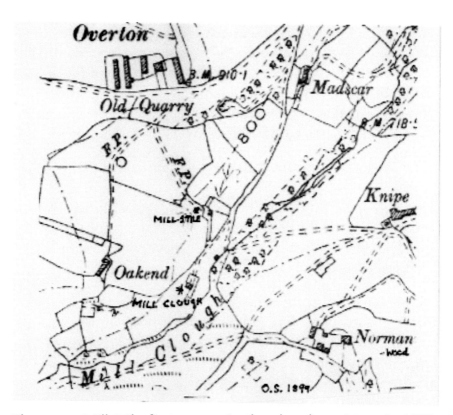

The name Mill Stile first occurs in the church registers in 1658. When the Jodrells attempted to auction off the Taxal estate at the Ram's Head in Disley in January 1832, the individual lots on offer included both a property described as Mill Stile and one referred to as Overton Mill dam, cottage. Both were occupied by Edward Heaps. The estate map drawn up for the auction expressly indicates a mill. Mill Stile is named, but two small buildings marked by the side of the mill pond, shown in blue, are not. On the tithe map, dating from 1844, Plot 152, Mill Stile, is described as a "Homestead etc." and its occupant as Edward's son, Joseph, who also rents plot 166, a long stretch of pasture running up the clough beside and beyond the pond. Two small buildings are again marked within the plot. J W Jodrell is owner and occupier of the pond itself, plot 153. A miniature volume of 1849 devoted to plans of farms belonging to the Jodrell Estate has John Pearson occupying Overton Mill, while Joseph Heaps is still at Mill Stile, as he is in the census of 1851. In

1871, in contrast, the Heaps are now living at Mill Clough.

A later photo of Mill Clough, showing John Wilson at the corner of the house and Sarah Ellen Wilson (1882-1896) on the roof of an outbuilding

In fact, Mill Stile does not figure at all in the census records for 1861, 1871 and 1881. In 1891 it is listed, but uninhabited. The evidence suggests that it was abandoned and the neighbouring mill or dam cottage rebuilt as a farm. All that now remains of Mill Stile is a little grassed-over mound in a field on the hillside.

The Heaps had lived at Mill Stile since 1809, when Edward Heaps succeeded George Turner there. After his death in 1824, the property was first taken on by his widow Betty and then by his son Joseph who had been christened at Taxal on February 13, 1802. Joseph married Martha Gaskell on 27 February 1827 and a son, the hero of our tale, Thomas Heaps, was christened at Taxal on 16 December. Martha died in 1831 and two years later Joseph married Elizabeth Kirk. In the 1841 census, he is recorded as living at Mill Stile with her, his two sons, Thomas (12) and George (10), a daughter Mary (7) and Elizabeth's daughter, Jane Kirk (9). He is described as a "powder labourer", as is Thomas. They must have both worked at the gunpowder mill at Fernilee. It was extremely dangerous work and in 1839 two of Joseph's brothers, George and Joseph, had been killed in a horrific explosion.[17] Elizabeth dies in March 1851 and Mary takes on the role of housekeeper. Not that Joseph is a widower for long: in 1853 he marries Emma Dunn from Manchester. In the 1861 census he is listed as a gunpowder maker and farmer of 6 acres living at Mill Clough. Thomas, on the other hand, has left the powder mill and is working as a timber feller and sawyer merchant. Foster Bower's now mature plantations were on his door step and guaranteed ample, much less dangerous work.

There is no way of knowing how Thomas adapted to his two step-mothers, but, what is beyond doubt is that he did not take kindly to what happened after Emma's death in February 1871, after which, according to my grandmother, "he treated old ladies to ¼lb of tea and a teapot." In the census held later that year the sole occupants of the farm are father and son, both listed as labourers. Joseph, with his appetite for female companionship still keen, soon finds a new partner, a washer-woman, who moves in with the pair. Relations between the three rapidly become fraught. On August 5 1871 the *Ashton Weekly Reporter* reports how Thomas, having been found guilty of stealing eggs from his aged father, had been sent to Knutsford gaol when unable to provide a pledge guaranteeing his future good behaviour. Friends leapt into the breach and he was released. But that was not the end of the affair. Someone had then broken in at Mill Clough and smashed up the washing machine. Joseph, suspecting his son to be the guilty one, had applied for him to be apprehended, but since he had no proof that Thomas had been near the farm, his application was rejected. Joseph died, aged 70, in the last quarter of 1871. My great-grandfather, John Morten, subsequently became the tenant of Mill Clough.

What happened to Thomas? Known as Monkey because of the mass of whiskers surrounding his weather-beaten face , he now worked as a general labourer at various farms. In the 1881 census he is living at the White Horse in Horwich End, in the 1901 census at Walker Brow Farm. My grandmother remembered him working for her father, who in the meantime had progressed from Mill Clough to Oakenend and thence to Sitch House.

There he slept in the corn chamber over the stable. With her sister and her brother she would peep through a crack in the door and listen to him saying his prayers. Invariably he would thank the Lord for his goodness to him and close with the words: "Thank you, Lord, for my warm bed."

Steps to a warm bed

He also worked for John's brother Henry at the Royal Oak, and it is photos taken there of him with his wheelbarrow that have preserved his image.

The coach house has not yet replaced what is left of the two cottages indicated on the map of 1849. Note also the lean-to attached to the church tower

"Monkey"

"Monkey" performed another important function. Whenever a local person died, he was summoned to the rectory and instructed to go to each farm in the valley to inform them who had died, together with the date and time of the funeral. After he had received one for the road at each stop, the clarity and accuracy of his message tended to suffer somewhat.[18] Thomas died in Macclesfield Workhouse, aged 77, in 1905. Such was the affection felt for him, that local farmers clubbed together to pay for his funeral at Taxal. He deserved it.

The last occupant of Mill Clough was Martha Lowe, a sister of Maurice Lomas's grandfather, Charles Lowe

Martha Lowe at Mill Clough with an unknown person

In this romantically eerie photo what seems a side door is in fact the front door. The wall was needed because of the very steep bank A single woman, Martha kept a pitchfork behind the door to deal with any unwelcome visitors. She was a terrible hoarder, but after her death in 1962, amidst a vast amount of junk, there was nothing of value except a pair of pistols. Without more ado the Water Board had the house knocked down.

Mill Clough in June 2021

Gone too are all but a few rusty remains of the hydraulic ram (pump) formerly housed in a little building by the bridge over the stream. In the 1950s we boys were fascinated by the distinctive noise it made as it pumped water up to Overton Farm.

So times change.

The Goyt valley could have looked very, very different from what it looks like today. In 1896 it was contemplated building a reservoir in Mill Clough, but it was not to be. Instead, one was built at Fernilee in the 1930s.

Tensions between tenants and landowner

The rent audits held at the Royal Oak continued throughout the century. On June 28 1879 the *Hyde and Glossop Weekly News* reported how on Tuesday last a capital meal had been provided there. Mr Nall, the Jodrells' agent, had collected the rents. He did the same at the Jodrell Arms. The fare consisted of beef, lamb, plum pudding and pastry. The proceedings afterward were, the report goes on, of a convivial nature and very agreeable.

John Nall and two other booted worthies. Nall's bowler hat reflects his position in the pecking order. With his two dogs, he alone is wearing gloves.

Behind the conviviality lay real tensions. In these depressed times farmers were often struggling to find their rents. Nall hoped that when they met again, "there would be better trade, not only with those engaged in trade itself, but also with farmers". No doubt, he went on, they had read in the newspapers recently something about landlords reducing their rents. He would have been very happy to follow suit if he had had instructions to do so. If an opportunity occurred to recommend a reduction or return of their rents, he would be most happy to use it. At present he could not tell how matters would stand. Nobody seems to have demurred. It needed real courage to speak up. The town clerk, Isaac Lomas, "a venerable old man" and one of those injured in the crash by the White Horse, lightened the mood by singing "Old Adam" to loud applause. It is not recorded whether this sensitive topic of rents was broached at the Royal Oak.

Disquiet with the Jodrells refused to go away. On September 16 1882, the *Hyde and Glossop Weekly News* contained an article by Antiquus entitled "Whaley and the Joderells", which was highly critical of them: having done their work and disappeared from the neighbourhood, they were, it alleged, to a great extent forgotten and unknown in the place where their own inherent abilities had lifted them head and shoulders above their fellows for many a hundred years. Financially they were people who had seen the main chance and used it to good purpose by all honourable means, including matrimonial transactions. Now they were conspicuous by their absence.

The *Manchester Evening News* took up the theme. On 6 July 1885 it carried an article on the farmers and their grievances. Having tried to silence them, Nall had angrily stomped out of a meeting at the Mechanics' Institute. A deputation was formed to wait upon him and ask for a reduction of 20%. Nothing less would be acceptable. If their reception was not satisfactory, the farmers would go direct to London and present their appeal there. A great many of the tenant farmers in the district, the article went on, say that they are very badly off and cannot continue much longer unless something is done. One farmer, who said he had been on his farm fifty years and been born there, could not find his rent even though there was just him and his son to keep. His proposal that they should all give notice was greeted with great acclamation. Another farmer said he - presumably his returns - had not paid one shilling towards his half-yearly rent: he had paid all of it out of his private resources. A postscript added that the promoters of the meeting hoped to hold others and hoped that by their actions they would secure financial advantages and other improvements, structural and others, on their holdings. This was a courageous step. "Troublemakers" risked being victimised or evicted. One wonders if there was any similar determination among the farmers gathered at the Royal Oak. I suspect that my great grandfather would have said nowt.

It was only when Sir Edward Cotton-Jodrell, who, like all those marrying into the Jodrell family, had to affix the Jodrell name to his own, came to live at Shallcross Hall and took a real interest in the estate that things looked up. My grandmother, whose opinion probably faithfully reflected her father's, was full of praise for his treatment of his tenants. Having taken to his bed, taking his whisky with him, John Morten died in 1917. His widow stayed on at the farm with her younger son Leonard, but once the farm had been sold at auction in November 1923 they were forced to leave. They moved to Kettleshulme, to a tiny farm, the Priest, just off the road going down to Kishfield. She died there in 1933, Lennie in 1950.

The one surviving picture of widowed Martha Morten, taken at Sitch House. Lennie is leaning over her shoulder. Sitting on her right is my grandmother with my father, Arthur, Mabel (standing), who later married Allan McLane, the Whaley Bridge surveyor, and Muriel (lying at the front), who married Jack Nall and ran Whaley Bridge post-office with him; on Martha's left is another daughter, Muriel Adelaide ("Addie") Morten, from Clayton Fold, with her son Frank, who later took over there from his father.

Sitch House in August 2021

The butter press
preserved at Sitch
House

During the reign of the Rev Samuel Evans

In 1887 the colourful "pugilistic parson", Samuel Evans bought the Taxal advowson and appointed himself rector. David Easton has excellently documented his doings and I can only recommend the reader to read about them on the website of the Furness Vale History Society.

At the Royal Oak things became difficult at the end of the 1880s. Henry Morten jun. died in 1889, and his widow soon got involved with the law. On 15 February 1890 the *Derbyshire Times* reported that the police had in their custody Mrs Morten, landlady of the Royal Oak, and a man named Pennington who had been living with her. The two were suspected of being involved in some burglaries which had recently been committed in the locality. Several houses in the neighbourhood had been broken into and suspicion was directed at the Royal Oak. When the police came to search the inn, Mrs Morten denied having seen Pennington for a fortnight, but he was found hiding upstairs.[19] Some of the stolen property was also found.

That was not the end of her woes. On June 14 the *Sheffield Independent* reported that the day before at New Mills County Court Messrs Barnard and Co, wine and spirit merchants in Buxton, had sued Lemuel King to recover £7 11s 10d for wines and spirits sold to him when he was in possession of the Royal Oak. His defence was that he was manager for his sister and not responsible for the debt. His honour gave judgement for the plaintiffs with costs. Another brewing company, John Gartside and Co, Ashton-under-Lyne, claimed £10.10s 0d from the same defendant and obtained a verdict in their favour. Death spared Mary any further trials. She was buried on July 25 1890.

Her late husband's youngest sister, Martha, took over the inn with her husband William Lomas. Things looked up.

Wedding Celebrations at the Royal Oak

On June 3 1892 the *Manchester Times* included a long feature entitled 'A holiday resort. Whaley Bridge and Taxal'.[20] It paints an idyllic picture:

> *The Royal Oak, a quiet little wayside resting place, with a little grey cottage or two, forms what there is of a village, and the old sexton and a rustic cottager, enjoying their afternoon chat in front of the open door with mine host of the "Oak", seem to comprise what there is of population. The Royal Oak, by the way, lays itself out for the entertainment of visitors, and every accommodation is provided.*

One could hardly have wished for better promotional material especially as a sketch accompanied the text:

Spot the difference from the photo

William died on August 9 1898, aged 68. Martha, much younger than her husband, lived on till November 18 1922. With her passing the line which had led from the Taylors, Colliers and Mortens to the Lomases was broken. It was left to the two cousins, my grandmother, Jessie Jackson, née Morten, and Martha's son, George, who farmed at Crowhill, to resurrect the Royal Oak's past whenever they met.

Notes

1   See *Derby Mercury*, 17.9.1834

2   *Sheffield Independent*, 31.7.68

3   *Hyde and Glossop Weekly News,* 27.7.78

4   This version of the story, taken from the *Derby Reporter*, appeared on 10 November in the *Carlisle Journal* under the heading "A premature interment"

5   An article entitled "The Extraordinary Parish of Taxal", published by the Furness Vale History Society, also looks at this incident.

6   See *Liverpool Standard* 22 & 29.5.55, *Manchester Courier* 25.1.78, *Manchester Times* 17.6.82, *Liverpool Mercury* 2.3.87.

7   Vegetarianism is dealt with in the book about Whaley Bridge

8   *Liverpool Standard* 24.11.65   .

9   *Derbyshire Courier* 15.5.40.

10   *Glossop Record* 13.8.64.

11   *Glossop Record* 15.11.65.

12   *Hyde and Glossop Weekly News* 2.9.71.

13   *Hyde and Glossop Weekly News,* 17.2.72.

14   *Derbyshire Courier* 15.10.61.

15   *Derbyshire Advertiser and Journal* 6.2.63.

16   *Hyde and Glossop Weekly News* 18.9.75.

17   See goyt-valley.org.uk/fernilee-powder-mill

18   See *Arthur Jackson Remembers,* Peartree Press, Whaley Bridge 1988, p 61.

19   *Sheffield and Rotherham Independent,* 14.2.90.

20   One can find a complete transcript of the article on the Furness Vale History Society website under the title "A Holiday Resort Whaley Bridge and Taxal"

Chapter 7
The changing face of Macclesfield Road

Basics

It is hardly surprising that I have always been fascinated by the history of Macclesfield Road. I did, after all, spend my boyhood at Nº 191 and have run and walked up and down it all my life.

Nº 191 must have been one of the smallest and most mod-con-free detached cottages in Whaley Bridge.

191 Macclesfield Road in the 1950s

In the kitchen a mantled gas light hissed high up in one corner - electricity, when it eventually came, was a revelation. A rough stone sink, fed only by a cold-water tap lay low down under the window. Lino covered an earthen floor. A square, walled "copper" for washing clothes - like the one in my grandmother's wash-house in Kettleshulme, but smaller - survived till my father came back at the end of the war and knocked it out. The mangle was outside by the coal-house. A galvanised tin bath was occasionally brought in from there and washed out before you gingerly negotiated its burning sides and squeezed into it. The WC - at least we didn't have an earth closet like the one in Kettleshulme - was part of an unlit block of three which also served 187 and 189. To reach it you had to negotiate, in all weathers, and at all times of the day, uneven and often very slippery stone flags. In the winter the water in the pan sometimes froze and the frosty wooden seat stuck to your bum. The *Daily Herald*, having provided instructive reading material, served another vital function. As the dividing walls were none too tight, pipe smoke and grunts from the middle cubicle betrayed the straining presence of Owen Bulmer, an elderly retired railway worker from Longsight or Levenshulme, who lodged at N° 189. At night a "jerry" did service.

The cottage, with a second roof added, is now double its original size. The tiny front garden, so lovingly tended by my mother, has gone to make way for a transit van. Progress comes at a price.

When I was 13, we moved down the road and rented N° 108 from my dad's uncle, Fred Jackson, who lived at N° 106. The piano was dragged down the road by heavier workmates like Joe Ford, and my dad's shed, once dismantled, followed, piece by piece. The washing and lavatorial arrangements remained basic, and the shed swallowed up the tiny piece of garden granted to us. In search of a decent-sized garden my parents moved to N° 100 in 1963. The shed continued its peregrinations - as did the piano. Even with a kitchen extension N° 100 was no paradise. A bath was rigged up in the loft, and a loo carved out of the front bedroom.

But the "lav" by the coal-house often remained the first port of call. A TV, a fridge and a phone came later. To the end my father resisted all talk of installing central heating. But there was the long garden and the glorious view. The view will, alas, soon be lost.

Housing development on Macclesfield Road has been an equally gradual, stuttering process.

The Dowry[1]

A coloured map of the Jodrell Estate captures the situation in 1830.

The then proud version of Taxal Lodge is indicated in red about half way up on the left. In the centre at the top one can see the old road to Macclesfield. It had been replaced as the main thoroughfare by the trunk road, which, off this map, turns up to the right before bending back round Mackintosh's Corner and going up along the side of Walker Brow.

At the junction of Macclesfield Road with the lane now known as the Rise, is a property marked 19a and, a little further along the lane, a larger building marked Dowery 21. In the register accompanying the tithe map of 1844 the former is described as "cottages etc", i.e cottages with gardens, occupied by Henry Pearson, the latter as a homestead occupied by George Pearson.

112

The tithe map also shows, diagonally across from the Linglongs, the cottage later numbered 191

Henry and George are the sons of Hugh Pearson (1742-1824) who had farmed at Crowhill. Widowed Nancy Pearson, 45, and her large family are its occupants in 1841. George, who has been at the Dowry at least since 1831, leases a number of fields; Henry does not.

In the census of 1841 only the occupants of one of the two buildings are recorded at the "Dowry": George and Ann Pearson and their two daughters, Hannah and Martha. He is listed,not as a farmer but only as an agricultural labourer - which reflects the place of this small farm in the hierarchy of farms. The cottages by the main road must, one assumes, be temporarily uninhabited.

On the 1849 map of Dowrey Farm George is listed as its lessee.

	Dowrey Farm George Pearsons						
12	House Building & Garden	e	1	10	e	e	23
13	Barn Croft	e	3	12	e	1	22
14	Town Place	1	3	10	0	3	17
15	Moor Field	2	e	17	e	3	39
16	House Field	1	2	7	e	2	46
17	Great Meadow	3	1	23	1	2	10
18	Mitchell Meadow	2	1	33	e	0	24
		13	1	23	3	3	17

He died in 1862, his wife in the following year. In the 1841 census the only other property at the Dowry is the present-day Nº 191. It is occupied by James Collier, a carpenter, who had married a Mary Pearson in 1832.They have two sons. He rents sever al fields in the direction of Taxal Lodge.

Following the example of his father, who had been both farmer and carpenter before taking on the Royal Oak, James combines the two roles. Sometime in the 1840s he moves on to a more substantial farm, Walker Brow, and is succeeded at the Dowry by his carpenter brother Charles and his family. In the 1861 census the cottage is specifically named Dowry Cottage.

While Charles is still at Dairy Cottage in 1871, there is no mention either here or later of Dowry or Dairy Farm, only of Dairy Lane Ends and Dairy Fold. Each is occupied by two households. At Dairy Lane Ends live George Pearson, 26, a quarryman, his wife Sarah 26 and two sons; John Williams, 37, a gamekeeper, lives next door. The occupants of Dairy Fold are, in the one cottage, George Pearson, 54, a quarryman, his wife Martha, 50, from Kettle-shulme, and two sons Hugh 17, a bleacher, and William 9, a scholar; in the other live the labourer Mathew Collier, familiar to us from the infanticide case, his wife and four children. These details all point to Dairy Lane Ends being the present-day N°s 172 and 174, while the two linked cottages next to Dowry Cottage, now N°s 193 and 195 - N° 197 is built on later - would seem to constitute Dairy Fold. For some reason - did it not have sufficient land to support it? - Dairy Farm must have been regarded as unviable and gradually fallen into disrepair. I can remember traces of it still surviving in the 1950s when we had our annual bonfire in the field at the end of the rough lane. Even they are gone now.

The Colliers' connection with the Dowry remained strong. At N° 191 we were tenants of Sidney (?) Collier in the 1940s and 1950s. Next door but one lived Ada Collier, a single woman who scuttled about, charring. Next to her were her brother, Frank, and his wife Ruth. In his clogs and with his snap-box tucked under his arm, Frank would clip-clop down the road on his way to work. Ruth played the piano at the Gospel Hall. Not that the Pearsons had gone entirely.

George William Pearson, a postman, was called up in the First World War but, physically unable to withstand the rigours of military life, subsequently discharged. The damage was done: he died in 1920 and lies buried at Taxal in a war grave. His widow, Helena, was a continual visitor at N° 191. In her slippers and with a heavy, black coat hanging like a vast tent right down to her ankles whatever the weather, she shuffled up and down the hill, clutching her walking-stick and shopping bag. Anyone she way laid, had a job getting away. She died in 1968, an unsung victim of the Great War.

Oxbent and Heybottom

Going down the hill from the Dowry, the first property one encounters on the 1830 map is in the area known as Oxbent. It is also the only one.

In 1841 two families are recorded as living there: that of Joseph Brown, 38, a stonemason, and that of Robert Wilson, 40, an agricultural labourer, one of whose sons, James, although only 8, is recorded as a bleacher. This would seem to indicate that he is working over the bridge at the Botany Bleach Works, which had opened in 1830. By 1844 both families have moved. Not far: in 1851 the Wilsons are living a little further down at Higher Heybottom, while the Browns are at Lower Heybottom

The road forks, with the main road going straight down to and across the Goyt, while the other fork bends to the right and ends at the river.

The map of 1830 shows Heybottom, i.e. the area running from below the beginning of Reddish Road and along the flat stretch to the Goyt, as containing three properties.

According to the 1841 census two families are living on the north side of the road: at the spot, roughly, where N° 43 stands today and at where N° 23 now is. The first is that of James Waring, 55, a tailor; the second, the large family of James Bottoms, 40, a collier. By 1844 George Brocklehurst has replaced him as the tenant. In both 1841 and 1844 the occupant of the house within the two forks of the road is Joseph Coleby . A "gentleman" and freemason from Adlington, and thus living close to the Jodrells, who lived at Henbury, he seems to have been invited by them to become their agent. Taxal Church records show a daughter born to him and his wife Ann at Whaley Bridge on 22 Feb 1794. Ann dies in 1805. He succeeds John Morten as the tenant of Lane Head Farm in 1795 and is listed in the Land Tax records for 1796 as also paying 10/– for Davenports, i.e Taxal Lodge. In 1797 Normanwood is added. Later Overton follows. He is listed as "Mr Coleby", whereas the other tenant farmers have first name and surname. Whoever was agent for the Jodrells, had considerable standing and clout in the area. Later he moved down to Heybottom and set up a nursery there. Indeed he was considered an expert in pruning. At some stage he was replaced as agent by Joseph Hudson Beswick of Macclesfield. He died in 1848, aged 83, and was buried at Taxal.

His daughter Harriet had married a man from Stockport or Bredbury called Charles Cheetham. In 1841 the couple are living at her father's. Charles, 45, is described as a nurseryman. In the 1851 census, in contrast, he is described as a schoolmaster; his wife as a mistress. The house is described as Taxal Cottage. Did they try to establish a school there? Did it fail? In 1861 Charles is recorded simply as a farmer of 5 acres and there is no mention of a school. He died on February 23 1868 and was buried at Taxal on the 27th. In the probate document his address is given as "Heybottom or Sunny Side." When I used to go down to wait at the Botany Mill gate for my father to emerge from the mill, a tiny, distant figure, from the mill, cross the cobbled yard and clock off at the lodge, I always ran past "Sunnyside". Used apparently by sub-managers at the mill, it seemed a mysterious place and anything but sunny, hidden as it was behind a forbidding high, dark stone wall. I never got a real look at it. It has long since to make way for industrial units. By the time the miniature volume containing plans of the farms on the Taxal Estate is published in 1849 , the lessee of the meadows at the front and rear of the Cheethams' house, as well as of the one and only property in Oxbent, is George Cawley. Living at Carr Cottage, he succeeded Beswick as the Jodrells' agent. Early in the 1860s he is dismissed and succeeded by John Nall

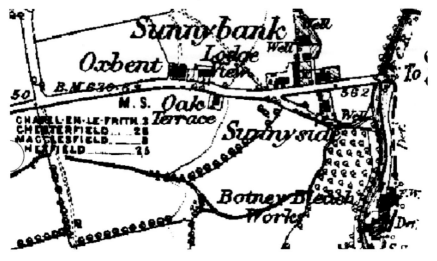

OS Map c 1875

Present-day N°s 25 to 49 have been built, and Oak Terrace and Lodge View (built in 1869) are indicated. Whereas houses on the north side of the road now go up to present-day N° 91, on the south side, Oak Terrace is still the limit. Built as an investment for the Taxal Burial Club, which met at the Royal Oak, these cottages were originally known as the Taxal Club Cottages - hardly an inspiring or endearing name. The nursery down at Sunnyside still survives on this map.

This crude drawing - made by whom and when and with how much regard to actual fact? - does at least give an impression of just how little housing had invaded the fields on both sides of Upper Macclesfield Road.

A copy which I have seen of the next photo has on the back the date, 1875. This may just be somebody's guess, but if the date is right, and it is a big if, Foresters' Row - in the centre - must have been built very soon after the O.S. map was completed.

The Twentieth Century

The O.S. map published in 1898 shows little change, but by the time its successor appears in 1910 houses now stretch from Oak Villas up to the present-day 80 or 82 and on the other side up to 115.

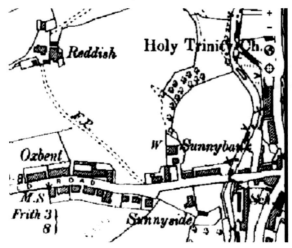

OS Map 1910. The nursery still survived

At the Dowry things have also changed.

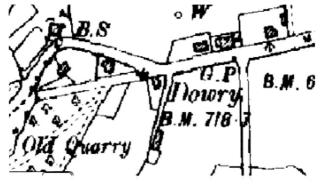

"Hill Top", "Kinrara" and "Woodside" are marked, and just below N° 191 are "Holly Bank", built in 1886, and "Moorlands" .The orchard in its large garden was visited in the 1950 by quite a few boys intent on scrumping - none too tasty - apples.

This postcard, one of which was posted in 1913, shows a further large house at the Dowry: "Brewood". Below the Linglongs one can see the side end of 140, Macclesfield Road. A builder called James William Wilson, who had married my grandfather Jackson's eldest sister Sarah, built 144-146 in 1916. I suspect he built the pair below, too. Just above Reddish Lane one can see the side end of N° 126. Below the lane leading across the fields to Taxal Lodge there seems to be a gap down to N° 112. One can make out the roof of N° 100. Across the road, the row beginning with N° 117 will be built in 1917. My good friends David and Lynne Hartley now live at N° 117.

The same view of a busy Macclesfield Road in September 2021

The following photo shows houses now going right up to Reddish Lane.

The next stage in the development of Macclesfield Road was a big one: the building of a large council estate in 1927. A stone was laid to mark the event. Taxal is still in Cheshire.

This is Upper Macclesfield Road today.

In the 1950s there was no need for car spaces. Harry Brookes's lorry might have been parked up at the top, and Mr Rowbotham at N° 134 could afford a posh car, but cars were rare. Macclesfield Road was yet to become the rat-run that it now is. The Kettleshulme bus, a tradesman's van, a coal-merchant's lorry, a motor bike, perhaps one with a sidecar, push bikes - they all might occasionally go past. Sam Longson's lime-covered lorries did come careering down round Mackintosh's Corner, but we had good warning of their approach and could still play "kicking in" with a tennis ball at the gate of N° 191 without having to interrupt play too often. Old Mr Slack's herd of cows had right of way. With full udders swinging from side to side, they filled up all the road and pavement as they plodded back to Reddish Farm. Their splattering plops, too runny to be collected as muck for the garden, studded the road. If Macc Road itself was quiet, Linglongs Road was a veritable paradise for hopscotch, skipping, cricket, tag, hide-and-seek, and riding about on trikes. Much of our lives as kids was spent playing outside, not sitting in front of TVs and video games or clutching mobile phones. The abandoned quarries at Walker Brow were our Mecca.

Developments at the Dowry

On this indistinct photo of the Linglongs one can just make out the houses on Macclesfield which are now numbered 187-197 and 172-174. That's all there is. Two pairs of semis will be built on the flat in 1933/34. After that a long lull ensues. Not until the 1950s is the lush meadow in front of N°s 191 - 197, with its wild flowers and the wonderful smell of freshly mown grass at hay-making time, dug up and built on. The signpost and the gas street-light disappear, as does the big board directing well-off urban diners in their cars across to the Chimes - or as one "all-made-up" female passenger, putting on a posh accent, pro-nounced it, the "Chimmes".

One by one bungalows start sprouting up along the left-hand side of the brow in the picture. They stop at the top and, supple-mented by houses, form Taxal Park as they work their way up to Taxal Edge and spread back towards Macclesfield Road. The last traces of Dowry Farm disappear for ever.

After the war the allotments on the reservoir side of the Dowry had become a wilderness. In the late 1940s and 1950s today's cult of allotments would have seemed a fantasy. Only William Heathcote ("owd Bill") and George Cook, the butcher at the

Co-op at Horwich End, still assiduously cultivated their islets in a sea of tangled fruit bushes and rampant weeds. In the 1950s they had to make way for another council estate. Johnny Ford's workshop and Reekies' hen run both disappeared. The brick tide lapped up against our sloping back garden at N° 191.

More estates

On this photo, which shows the prefabs built on Park Road after the Second World War, one can still see the meadows below Reddish Lane and to the side of Macclesfield Road. The prefabs are followed by council houses and then themselves demolished to make way for old people's bungalows. The meadows disappear at the end of the 1980s under the estate known as Mereside Gardens.

For a while all was quiet. But then, out of the blue, came the fiercely but ultimately vainly challenged plan to build over 100 houses and flats on the fields stretching down from the Linglongs towards the Botany.

Until a year ago this was the peaceful scene between Lomas's Knob, the Linglongs, Macclesfield Road and the track leading to Taxal Lodge. At the top we played cricketon our tufty, unmown, often cow-pat pocked pitch, and dammed up the little stream winding down by the trees. Our pitch has disappeared under house foundations, and the proud oak at the top of the photo, a tree that had stood for so long in the centre of the field, has sadly been chainsawed out of its peaceful existence.

Building stopped play. Two leafy escapees look on in silence in August 2021

One wonders how long it will be before a vast estate swallows up the broad, prime fields running up from the top of the Linglongs to the Nursery and Moor Road. How long will the rushy, unmutilated side of Lomas's Knob continue to stretch across to Taxal Lodge and the old driveway? And what will become of the Lodge itself and its grounds? Will the deer and badgers disappear for ever? Will the ghosts of the many kids who once delighted in sledging there still be able to re-enact their chilly exploits on the various slopes between "Kinrara", the reservoir and the allotment council houses?

Note

1 See Dave Dusgate, *Dowry – a settlement in the Parish of Taxal,* 1998. This booklet written for the Whaley Bridge Amenity Society thoroughly researches the whereabouts at the Dowry of the Pearsons and Colliers. We sometimes reach different conclusions.

Part 2 and Part 3

of

Stepping into the past

are on their way

Part 2 is devoted to

Kettleshulme

Chapters include: An early Victorian athlete; A mystery solved – Moses Jackson's crime and fate; Creating a community centre - from Library to Memorial Hall; Fake news and parish - pump politics - the case of the Earl of Rock Savage; Victorian self-help - The Oddfellows Friendly Society; Burning effigies - church and chapel at war? Chalk and cheese - two very different Anglican curates.

Part 3 is devoted to

Whaley Bridge

Chapters include: Struggling to survive - the White Hart; Taking on the tipplers - the Band of Hope; Roast beef under fire - the Vegetarian Society; In search of social stability - the founding of the Mechanics' Institute; Queen Victoria's Home Guard - the Rifle Volunteers; The rise and fall of the village postmaster.